The Edinburgh Pub Guide

Polygon

© Polygon 1989
22 George Square, Edinburgh

Printed in Great Britain by
Bell & Bain Ltd
Glasgow

British Library Cataloguing
   in Publication Data

The Edinburgh Pub Guide
1. Edinburgh. Public Houses
647'.954134

ISBN 0 7486 6053 4

TEXT & COVER DESIGN by Art Dept. EDINBURGH
Typeset by Waverley Graphics Ltd., Edinburgh.

CONTENTS

EDITOR'S INTRODUCTION

Since the last guide was published by Polygon nearly ten years ago, Edinburgh's pubs have changed considerably. The brewing industry in Scotland, especially that of the capital, has seen radical changes also. The number of individual breweries has continued to shrink and the six big companies have consolidated their hold over the market. The result of this has been a loud shriek of complaint from the real ale enthusiasts who want a return to natural methods of brewing and delivery. They have had some success: breweries do encourage some outlets to take cask-conditioned beers and the foundation of the Rose Street Brewery shows that small breweries can, in exceptional circumstances, survive.

But the average consumer is not a real ale enthusiast and publicans have become more sensitive to their demands, partly because of a growth in disposable income over the last ten years. In general, people are no longer content with pubs that cater only for men who congregate in the evenings to drink beer and whisky. They want a more comfortable place to sit, clean surroundings and quick service. Women are forming an increasingly large portion of the market so landlords have begun to stock a wider range of products.

Patterns of behaviour have also changed. People travel more and are exposed to different cultures and products: they demand new, cosmopolitan drinks from their pubs. More money is spent on eating out these days. Pubs therefore make a much bigger effort to provide good food and few rely only on their drinks earnings. Lunch-time custom has become more important.

Despite the bourgeoisification of many pubs, folk culture and local loyalty is still closely associated with public houses. Edinburgh is fortunate not to have allowed town planners to draw the pub out of their blueprints for an ideal society.

This pub guide does not claim to be comprehensive. Many favourite pubs have probably been left out. What we have tried to do is include as many varieties of pubs as possible: wee howffs, hotel lounges, family inns, theme bars, spit and sawdust locals and so on. We have kept a special eye on pubs that have opened recently or have been refurbished. So whether you are an Edinburgh resident who has grown up with your local boozer, a visitor searching for the soul of the City, or just a pub enthusiast with a strong sense of curiosity, then you should find what you are looking for.

James Bethell.

THE BREWING INDUSTRY IN EDINBURGH

by Charlie McMasters, the Brewing Industry's Archivist at Heriot Watt University, Edinburgh

Until recent years, the brewing industry dominated Edinburgh as did no other, bestriding streets such as the Canongate, Fountainbridge and Holyrood Road, and dominating the entire city by its presence. For many a first-time visitor to Edinburgh their most immediate sensation upon alighting from a train at Waverley Station was the all-pervasive smell of the breweries wafting up from the Canongate. When viewed from vantage points such as Calton Hill or the Salisbury Crags, Edinburgh revealed itself as a veritable forest of belching brewery chimney stacks which, along with the attended slatted-and-louvred brewhouses and pagoda-roofed malt kilns, made for a distinctive skyline.

Nowadays, in large parts of Edinburgh, the industry which was once the lifeblood of the local community is now a thing of the past. There are now only three breweries remaining in Edinburgh, plus one pub brewery, whereas twenty years ago there were four times that number. All the surviving breweries are to the west of the city centre, the last of the Old Town breweries having closed its doors in 1986. When once the streets of Edinburgh's Old Town would be full of brewery workers, coopers, draymen, maltmen, mashmen, kilnmen and copper-head men, the streets are now strangely silent, except for the tourists and the passers-by. The smell of malt and hops has gone also.

Although thought of as primarily a distilling nation, Scotland has in fact a long and proud brewing tradition which stretches back far beyond that of distilling. It is known that the Picts were noted brewers and that before the arrival of the Romans, Scots brewed using heather, rowan and broom. By the early Middle Ages, brewing was being secretly practiced by the religious orders—the monks of Holyrood are known to have been brewing ale in the twelfth century.

Within a couple of centuries, the secularization of brewing took place, and brewing became a widespread domestic industry, often practiced in the home of women. Most brewers could only produce enough for immediate needs, but by the fifteenth century 'publick' brewers, that is commercial brewers, began to make an appearance. In Edinburgh, a powerful Society of Brewers was formed as early as 1598, to control the supply of good brewing waters and malting barley, and by the 1700s commercial brewing was well established in Edinburgh, particularly in the Canongate, Pleasance and Grassmarket areas. Some of the most important names in Edinburgh brewing history were established at this time such as Dryborough, Younger and Campbell.

The excellence of Edinburgh beers could be attributed to the 'Charmed Circle', an underground channel of fine hard brewing water which ringed the city. By the 1880s, Edinburgh could boast some forty breweries, but from this peak the numbers began to steadily decline, with a trend towards larger units leading to an inevitable rationalisation and elimination of breweries. By the end of the Second World War the number had more than halved from the peak at the turn of the century. As late as 1960, Edinburgh still had 16 breweries but that decade proved to be a locust period and the industry was decimated.

Despite its huge contraction, the brewing industry has left an indelible mark on Edinburgh, and its legacy can be seen everywhere, from the ancient Abbey Brewery on Horse Wynd to the derelict Argyll Brewery on the Cowgate, and from the now-silent Holyrood Brewery on the Royal Mile, to the ill-fated and forbidding Bell's Brewery on the Pleasance. It is now a far cry from the days when Edinburgh could lay claim to being the brewery capital of the world, but Scottish and Newcastle, with its head offices and Fountainbridge Brewery in Edinburgh, remains Scotland's biggest manufacturing company.

And so to the beers. The three breweries, Fountain (McEwan's), Heriot (Tennents) and Caledonian (Caledonian) produce a range of ales, beers and lager. McEwan's and Tennents 70/- and 80/- in their various forms are widespread, and both these breweries also produce lagers.

The third brewery, the Caledonian Brewery, produces a range of traditional unpressurized cask beers only and no lager. The other Scottish breweries products, those of Belhaven, Maclays, Broughton and Alloa, can be found in Edinburgh pubs, with the products of the tiny Traquair and Harviston Breweries.

The shilling system of categorisation, refers merely to the old invoice price per barrel, but is nowadays merely an indication of ascending strengths. Many free and brewery-tied houses now sell a range of beers including English 'guest' beers not commonly available in Scotland. Indeed, to find discerning Scots drinking (and even enjoying) English beers is a phenomenon virtually unthinkable ten years ago.

At some of Edinburgh's best real-ale bars, the Malt Shovel, the Southsider, or Bannerman's, the choice of beers is quite staggering. Edinburgh is still a good place to drink, although a bit on the pricey side. Bars such as the Cafe Royal, Bennet's Bar, or the Abbotsford can be relished for their architecture, while weel-kent Edinburgh hostelries such as the Athletic Arms or Mathers Bar can be appreciated for their ambience and their beers.

Despite the closure of several local breweries over the last few years, there is little doubt that drinkers in Edinburgh now have more choice than they did at the beginning of the decade. Distinctive Scottish beers continue to be produced. Try the Caledonian, Belhaven or Maclays range of cask beers, or, for a bottled beer, Fowlers Wee Heavy or McEwan's Blue Label. And for those of you who like lager, our homegrown Tennent's Lager reached its centenary recently, and continues to have a strong and loyal following. The licensing changes of the last few years allowing pubs to be open all day have made for many an illicit and convival afternoon refreshment, and really, what could be better?

COMMON SEAL OF EDINBURGH.* (*After Henry Laing.*)

COUNTER SEAL OF THE ABOVE.† (*After Henry Laing.*)

INTRODUCTION TO THE OLD TOWN

In places it may be dingy, shabby and not a little dangerous to walk in after dark, nevertheless, the Old Town is an area of Edinburgh with as much to offer as befits its colourful past.

The Old Town can roughly be defined as that part of Edinburgh enclosed by the Old Flodden Wall, built following the disastrous battle of the same name in 1513. The wall ran from the south-east corner of the Castle rock, across the bottom end of the Grassmarket, along and around Greyfriar's Kirk, by the present site of the University, then turning north again close to the Pleasance. Here a section of the wall can still be seen today. From there, it goes north to where Waverley Station now stands, eventually linking up with the Nor' Loch (which was later drained to create Princes Street Gardens).

Within this area over the centuries, we find a wealth of characters, events, interesting architecture and, more recently, pubs. For even though today much of the fame of the Grassmarket and the Royal Mile rests on the high frequency of pubs there, in days of yore, this was the part of town that provided residences for the likes of David Hume, James Boswell and the notorious Deacon Brodie; the part of the town that included such notable buildings as the Scottish Parliament House in which the 1707 Act of Union was fiercely debated, John Knox's house, St Giles Cathedral and the Castle. Of course, many of these buildings are still visible today, and indeed, their splendour and importance has been re-emphasised by the nastier aspects of the Old Town in the 20th century.

A great favourite among the more adventurous pub-goers is to 'do the Royal Mile'. So, on the stretch of road that kings and queens once passed along from the Castle to Holyrood Palace, sorry bands of wastrels can be spotted, winding their weary way from pub to pub in an attempt to sample the alcoholic delights of each and every establishment on the Mile—and there are quite a few.

Down below lie the Grassmarket pubs, copious and more or less one of a kind: simplistic, undemanding and at the weekend, packed to the gunnels. The Grassmarket leads into the Cowgate, traditionally regarded as the place for late-night drinking in less than tasteful surroundings. Recently though, the east end of the Cowgate has undergone something of a renaissance, with new blocks of flats, chic cafe-bars and the yuppiefication of nearby Blair Street.

The mixture of the dingy, the comfortable, the trendy and the developing typifies not just the state of licenced premises in the Old Town but also the state of the Old Town as a whole. Classic tenements and halls mingle with refurbished, upmarket flats, old closes yawn between restaurants, pubs and shops, while further to the west, the plastic wine bars and tacky extremes of Lothian Road bars stand side-by-side with such imposing structures as the Lyceum Theatre and the Usher Hall. This, and lots more besides, is what the Old Town offers residents and visitors.

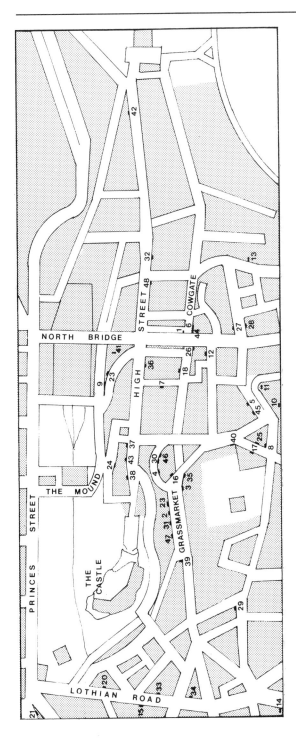

THE OLD TOWN

1. Bannerman's
2. The Beehive
3. Bo's Bar
4. The Bow Bar
5. The Bistro
6. Cafe Coste
7. The City Café
8. Doctor's
9. The Doric Tavern
10. The Teviot Union
11. The Potterrow Union
12. The Chamber Street Union
13. The Pleasance Union
14. The Cameo
15. The Filmhouse
16. The Traverse
17. The Forrest Hill Bar
18. The Green Tree
19. The Junction Bar
20. Joe's Garage
21. L'Attache
22. The Last Drop
23. The Malt Shovel
24. Oblomov
25. Oddfellows
26. The Pelican
27. Rutherford's
28. Stewart's Bar
29. Tap-O-Lauriston
30. Trader Vic's
31. Black Bull
32. The Blue Blanket
33. The Bull and Bush
34. The Burnt Post
35. Candlemaker Arms
36. Covenanter's
37. Deacon Brodies
38. Ensign Ewart
39. Fiddler's Arms
40. Greyfriar's Bobby
41. The Halfway House
42. Jenny Ha's
43. The Jolly Judge
44. The Kasbar
45. Negotiants
46. The Preservation Hall
47. The White Hart
48. The World's End

9

BANNERMAN'S
55 Niddry Street, The Cowgate

Bannerman's has all the characteristics pub reviewers search for: 'coziness', 'atmosphere', 'comfort'. The difference here is that it offers all these appealing features while resembling a vaulted crypt lurking in the inky-black shadows of the towering South Bridge, which looms overhead dripping moisture into the road below.

Step inside and the image continues: long, Transylvanian Castle-like tables, low stone archways, the ominous sounding 'Red Room', a toilet lurking at the end of the corridor with standing room for hunchbacks only. All this is only part of Bannerman's charm, for this is a place where connoisseurs of 'real ale' mumble softly to themselves, their eyes go misty, hands fumble and shake as a cornucopia of liquid delight appears before them: Arrols 80/-, Caledonian, Tetley's Bitter, Burton Ale, Beamish Irish Stout—all of them cask conditioned and hand-pulled.

As for bottled beers, Bannerman's is one of the few pubs in Edinburgh to serve fruit beers flavoured with cherry, raspberry or banana, as well as Ziefman's Greek beer. On top of this, there are 35 whiskies to chase down those real ales.

Reinforcing the notion that most real ale drinkers are folkies with beards and thick jerseys is the regular crowd that gathers in the 'Red Room' on Monday and Tuesday nights to hear live folk music. But the folkies are not the only punters attracted to Bannerman's. The extremely cheap lunches draw in office workers and students, others come for the jazz on Thursdays, others come simply to sample the experience of sitting on rickety old chairs around huge barrels.

THE BEEHIVE
18-20 The Grassmarket

Follow the steps down from the Castle to the Grassmarket and you'll find yourself beside The Beehive, a fine old Edinburgh house in the shadow of Edinburgh's mighty fortress. The beautiful building in which The Beehive is housed dates back to the 17th Century. The thistle motif outside is a relic from the Corn Exchange building which once stood opposite, a reminder to us to treasure the historic buildings which still stand in the Grassmarket.

Once lured into the warm confines of The Beehive, the visitor is in surroundings of the utmost taste with sepia photographs of the city providing good topics for conversation.

The Beehive does have a very good range of ales including Theakstons' Best Bitter and Old Peculiar, Younger's No. 3, Tennent's L.A., along with cask-conditioned McEwan's 70/- and 80/-. Lunches are available at the bar for around £2.50 or else you can try The Beehive restaurant next door.

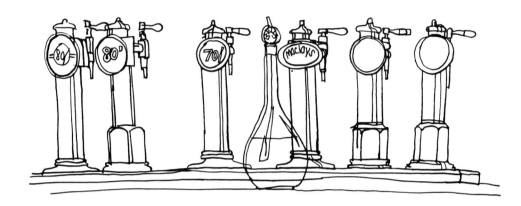

BO'S
Bo's Bar, High Street
Black Bo's, Blackfriars Street

It is a mere eighteen months since Bo's Bistro, the first Bo's, opened up in the Grassmarket. Since then, Bo's Bar has appeared in the High Street, and more recently, Bo's Diner and Black Bo's in Blackfriars Street.

Bo's Bar is small and intimate with large round tables fitted into a thin room. It is very much a place to sit around for hours talking and drinking. Black Bo's is also relaxed and friendly, but has more of a potential for a pub atmosphere than Bo's Bar. The decor of Black Bo's is an example of the style of pub design which is very much in vogue these days: bric-a-brac collected personally by owner Alex Nicholson covers the walls, including such oddments as a skipping rope strung across the roof.

If the atmosphere of Bo's is down-to-earth and honest, then the bar prices are equally so. Drinks served by friendly staff are very reasonably priced, the basic pint costing £1. Bo's Diner and Bo's Bistro are also recommended for their good food, with main courses at around £5.

THE BOW BAR
Victoria Street

The Bow is the sort of pub you would expect to find on Victoria Street. It fits in perfectly with all the traditional, nostalgic shops which surround it, and like them, it believes in quality as a means of attracting customers. Unlike its cosy atmosphere, however, its history is rather more lively.

In the 1670s, there was a temple on the site where Major Thomas Weir, lay preacher, devil worshipper and self-styled 'Wizard' used to ply his trade. This was not much appreciated by Edinburgh's up-standing citizens, who eventually burnt him at the stake. He became known as the

'Bowhead Saint' and the first Bow Bar appeared in 1860.

Nowadays, the pub is well-known for its huge selection of whiskies and beers. There are an astonishing 128 malts available and seventeen grains, as well as nine different cask beers, including the more unusual London Pride. They also stock twenty different rums. There is a good selection of food too: Forfar bridies, steak and mince pies, as well as filled rolls and salads. With newspapers available at the bar, this is a good place to while away a lunch-hour.

The Bow's decor is also indicative of the pub's old-fashioned quality. The walls are wood-panelled, with a beautifully engraved gantry and bar. Original advertising signs and mirrors cover the rest of the pub, and all this makes for a homely, peaceful atmosphere, especially as there is no jukebox or fruit machine.

THE BRISTO BAR
41 Lothian Street

This bar's location on the edge of the University's George Square makes it a popular student venue. In particular, the local sports clubs find at the Bistro the right combination of unbreakable fittings and late-night opening for their drunken tom foolery in the evenings.

The bar is decorated with robust wood panels and, quite strangely, satellite TV. In the afternoon, everyone stops to watch Neighbours and at the weekend the armchair athletes rest in front of Grandstand until the serious drinking starts later on.

At night, the noise of screaming centre-forwards and singing flankers makes the place almost unbearable, but a large selection of malt and Irish whiskies, and the good beer which includes Belhaven 90/- and Beamish Stout make up for it.

CAFÉ COSTE
Robertson's Close, The Cowgate

Café Coste opened in March 1989 below a new block of university flats, and despite the rather garish blue hue of the building, the interior of the pub itself is tasteful. It may be typical of a general trend towards a continental style of decor (Oblomov and L'Odeon are two other Edinburgh examples), but it is refreshing nevertheless.

Friendly staff, cheerful atmosphere and the club nights often do more than compensate for the prices, (just a touch too expensive) and the lack of any significant departures from the norm in the way of beers, lagers and shorts on offer. But the icing on the cake must be the Sunday morning experience: food, coffee, newspapers, ambience. Sheer bliss. As for weekdays, Café Coste is the perfect place for a cosmopolitan morning coffee and croissant. You could almost be on the terrace of a café on the Champs Elysee (if it were not for the lack of a terrace . . .)

At present, Café Coste is an invigorating experience in a steadily improving area of the town. If you like your cafe-bars a bit more sophisticated than your average 'charming wee howff', then go continental at Café Coste.

THE CITY CAFÉ
19 Blair Street,
off the High Street

Despite its rather clinical and unwelcoming exterior, this is an unusual and central café offering continental food and drink. Chrome and black furnishings create a 1950s atmosphere, helped along by the appropriately dressed bar staff. You can choose to sit conspicuously at the spotless bar or preferably retreat to one of the diner-style booths.

Although quiet and airy during the day, this is one of the places to be seen at night, with a fair amount of serious posing going on. The usual crowd is lively, consisting of arty, studenty types with the odd fashion designer thrown in. At the bar, there is bottled beer and lager plus the usual on draught. If you cannot face another drink, go for the excellent coffees and hot chocolate, served until closing time at 1am.

Dinner is also available late (5.30-11pm Monday-Thursday, 5.30-12 midnight Friday & Saturday, 6.30-10.30 Sunday), including Italian dishes and salads. For the sweeter tooth, pastries, icecreams, milkshakes and confectionary can be had all day. On Sunday, the speciality is the brunch menu, a bit of a luxury at £4.95 from noon-3pm. Bar open 12-1am Monday-Saturday, 6.30-11pm Sunday.

DOCTORS
corner of Teviot Place and Forest Road

Appropriately named, this pub is situated opposite the medical school and just along from the Royal Infirmary Hospital. It has recently been redecorated in an attempt to attract a more 'up-market' clientele. However, it is frequented, as it always has been, by hospital workers from porters to surgeons.

The interior is a strange mixture of new velvet trimmings and the subtle lighting of wine bars, and old relics of medical equipment which adorn the walls and give this place the hint of history which it deserves. The most attractive features are the booths.

Owned by Scottish and Newcastle Breweries, it has their brews available as well as Theakstons' Best Bitter, Old Peculiar and Greenmantle on draught.

Despite the fact that the ambience is pleasant and the music is provided by customers who want to play their tapes, theis pub lacks character and is 'clinical' in this respect. Opening hours are 11am-11pm Monday-Wednesday. 11am-Midnight Thursday. 11am-1am Friday and Saturday. 6.30pm-11pm Sunday.

THE DORIC TAVERN
McGUFFIE'S BAR
15 Market Street

Housed in an old tenement building, The Doric is an inconspicuous but extremely popular pub and a restaurant. Its well-worn wooden interior is shady and intimate. Being sandwiched between the City Art Centre and the Fruitmarket Gallery has made it a haven for artists and culture vultures. The nearby Scotsman offices also supply a regular flow of journalists and businessmen.

The bar has a wide range of malt whiskies and a good selection of wines, with a pint of Caledonian 80/- at around £1.15. In the ever-crowded restaurant, expect to pay £6.50 for a 3-course set menu (Mon.-Sat.) of good quality, unusual food including steaks, fish and a good choice of vegetarian dishes. Inoffensive light jazz and classical background music also make it a good coffee stop.

This is a small pub so be prepared for an intimate late-night atmosphere. Downstairs in McGuffie's, the beer is cheaper at £1 a pint and the feel of the place is more cosy and friendly, with darts, dominoes and a jukebox. Definitely a working man's pub with a lot of regulars from Waverley Station.

"STOOD UP?"

EDINBURGH UNIVERSITY UNIONS
Teviot, Potterrow, Chambers Street, Pleasance

The University has four main areas all of which are well used by those attending the Fringe Festival during the summer.

Starting off with the biggest: Teviot Row, the oldest purpose-built student union in Britain, is an imposing gothic pile of sandstone turrets containing three bars, carvery, canteen-type restaurant and pizza bar, as well as two discos. The most popular of all the unions, on Fridays it becomes a loud cattle-market, a nightmare setting of neon, music and hopelessly drunk students from all over Edinburgh. During the week though, Teviot Row is an ideal place for a very cheap meal or an equally cheap and quiet drink.

Then there is Potterrow, situated under the dome of the Mandela Centre. Smaller, 'cosier' and an altogether nicer atmosphere than Teviot, Potterrow is frequented by the

more 'alternative' among the student body. Again, the food is cheap but basic, with the drink cheaper than Teviot's.

During the day, Chambers Street is mainly visited by students from the nearby law faculty, and offers much the same as the other unions in terms of food and drink. As host of the popular Rock Night, Chambers Street is a (un)happy medium between the two extremes of Teviot and Potterrow.

Finally, the Pleasance Bar is not strictly speaking a Union, but is the most pleasant of all the bars—comfy seats, an open fire, often a jazz band playing.

Entry to the Unions varies depending on the day of the week, and may depend on production of a matriculation card, although during the Festival, Teviot becomes the Fringe Club, a late night haven of drinking, eating and entertainment for all. As for the cost of entry, during term-time the policy is somewhat confused, but expect to pay a nominal charge.

CAMEO CINEMA
38 Home Street
228 4141

Small and spartan, the Cameo Bar is fine for a pre-film drink, although the selection is rather limited. The cinema itself is worth a visit though. Bar open 6-11.30pm Monday-Saturday.

FILMHOUSE
88 Lothian Road
228 6382

The Filmhouse is busy with people seeing films or just out for a drink. It is also a welcome change from the loud, impersonal regular Lothian Road pubs. The much-missed restaurant is due to re-open in the summer but the bar itself is comfy and friendly. Open 12.30-11pm Monday-Saturday, 6.30-11pm Sunday.

TRAVERSE THEATRE
Grassmarket, bottom of Victoria Street
226 2623

The Traverse's newly-opened bar and restaurant is a good alternative to the Grassmarket pubs, offering very reasonable food from 11am-7.30pm, Tuesday-Saturday and 6.30-7.30 Sunday, £2-£2.50 for unusual vegetarian dishes and under £2 for a quiche with salad. The bar serves 70/-and 80/- and a large selection of wine. Arty but informal decor and a lively atmosphere make it very popular with students and shoppers as well as theatre-goers. Open 10.30am-2am Tuesday-Saturday and 6-11pm Sunday, during Festival.

FORREST HILL BAR
Known as SANDY BELL'S
25 Forrest Hill

The history of the folksong revival in Scotland is inextricably bound up with the chequered career of Sandy Bell's bar (or the Forrest Hill Bar, to give it its official title). Back in the 40s, Sandy's was a Medical School howff, never without its quota of Gaelic-speaking Hebrideans, and it was still privately owned by a family called Bell. Shortly after World War II, the last of the dynasty, Miss M.C. Bell, engaged a relative called Sandy—the very image of a genial, garrulous, rubicund barman—to look after the pub, and by what was, in the circumstances, an appropriate folk process, his name and Bell's became conjoined. The result was so obviously right that it caught on.

After the foundation of the School of Scottish Studies in 1951, Sandy Bell's became its 'local' (though which was the HQ and which was the annexe has sometimes been disputed!) In the same year, the first of a series of 'People's Festivals' took place, and the centre-piece of this was an epoch-making ceilidh of authentic traditional singers, Gaelic and Scots. From then on, Sandy Bell's found itself in the midst of a veritable explosion of creative 'folk' activity, and it was in it that the late, great Jeannie Robertson, generally accounted the finest Scots ballad-singer of modern times, enjoyed her Edinburgh debut.

In the mid 50s, the Edinburgh University Folksong Society came into existence; its first (unofficial) HQ was also Sandy Bell's. The guiding spirit was an exceedingly gifted medical student called Stuart Macgregor, a singer-songwriter as well as a promising novelist. The heady atmosphere of those days is vividly evoked in Stuart's first novel *The Myrtle and Ivy* (1967). His photo, and a copy of his tender, comic lovesong 'The Sandy Bell's Man', hang in a place of honour near the fireplace.

The pub is still the folk music centre for discriminating afficionados, and (as always) the sessions are spontaneous—never organised. There is no juke-box. Why not drop in—and gie's a sang!

THE GREEN TREE
182-184 Cowgate

Gone are the days when you might have caught Swamptrash filling the place with picto-cajun kick-ass thrash, but this square, island-barred pub still has live music on Mondays and Thursdays (and no piped music or juke box). The ceiling beams are fibreglass and the fire in the grate is gas-powered—even the cracks and holes in the walls are painted on (very convincingly)—but the atmosphere is genuine enough, especially at weekends during term time, when the wooden benches are just distant memories for most of the clientele. There is a big, fairly sheltered twenty-table courtyard for the summer, the hours are 11.00-02.00 (18.30-23.00 Sundays), the beers are Belhaven 80/-, Special and Lager, Tennent's Lager, Murphy's and Beamish, plus the usual bottles of Newky Brown and Grolsch, as well as Red Stripe. There may well be a guest beer too, by the time you

read this. Rioja by the glass is a nice touch. Food is soup, stovies (by the bowl: tasty, cheap and filling), generous rolls, open sarnies, and salads (no food on Sundays). Public telephone, fag machine, no TV, one quiet fruit machine, chess and doms available. Handy for Wilkie House and the Gilded Balloon, but worth visiting for its own sake. Deserves its popularity.

THE JUNCTION BAR
269 Great Junction Street

Formerly the Blackwood, this pub has come under new management and has returned to its original name of the days when the tram cars used to terminate their run close by. The removal of the false ceiling in the bar, together with the considerable refurbishment which has been tastefully done, has returned the style and old fashioned ambience it knew in former years. The wooden beams, low ceilings, open fireplace and candles in the lounge give a strong homely atmosphere—akin to that of a country pub.

Both lounge and bar have an effectively cluttered decor with swords, old lamps, antlers (even a royal deer's head), books, bottles, murals, pictures, pub mirrors and a proliferation of comic cartoons drawn by a local artist, depicting local events and mishaps.

The full range of Alloa ales is served and the pub specialises in the Auld Reekie 90/- brought from the Rose Street Brewery. This pub is one of the six outlets for this ale of 1056 specific gravity fame. In addition, Lowenbrau and Swan low alcohol lagers are on draught.

The food served here is more than just standard pub lunches with haggis amongst other things on the menu. Visitors residing in nearby Bed & Breakfast use this place as a restaurant. Folk nights are held on Fridays especially during the summer months.

Seventeen satellite channels are available on the TV in the public bar. There is a CD juke box in the lounge. Darts, dominoes, Trivial Pursuit, backgammon and chess are also available to customers.

The pub sponsors five sporting teams and a 2CV rally car. The clientele is a harmonious, heterogenous mix from students to working folk. The atmosphere is relaxed and friendly, the proprietor extends great hospitality to both regulars and newcomers. Highly recommended.

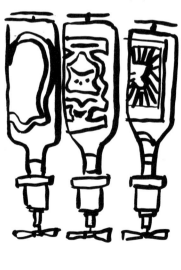

JOE'S GARAGE
Lothian Road

Does uniqueness necessarily make a good pub? A visit to Joe's Garage at the bottom of Lothian Road will convince you that it does not. For though this pub is a wonder to behold—the garage theme (surprise, surprise) even stretches to the inclusion of two whole cars and a phone-box—as a drinking establishment, it is hardly captivating.

For a start, it is not cheap—when I visited I was charged £1.40 for two halfs of Becks. And then there is the clientele: very 'laddish' and often with an undercurrent of tension sadly all too typical when groups of young males gather to consume large quantities of lager. One ex-member of staff spoke of the frequent patronage of the pub by a troop of gurkhas and the prostitutes that trailed in their wake.

But it's not all bad. Aptly enough, as an old car showroom, Joe's Garage has huge front windows that are drawn aside in warmer weather and during the Festival, pavement artists are invited into this opened-up area to practice their act. On these occasions, Joe's Garage can be very pleasant indeed, but equally it has the potential to be very unpleasant. Whatever the instance, remember to take a lot of money.

L'ATTACHE
Rutland Street

L'Attache on Rutland Street is a popular West End wine bar with a warm and relaxed feel. Converted from hotel cellars only three years ago, the brickwork and stone arches of L'Attache create quite an atmosphere, whilst dim lighting and a pleasantly cluttered arrangements lend intimacy to a place which is, in fact, fairly spacious.

There is a strong policy for live entertainment at L'Attache. Local jazz and folk bands appear frequently with jazz every Wednesday night and Sunday afternoon. Drink prices are not cheap with wine upwards of £6 per bottle and Beck's Bier coming in at £1.50 a pint.

L'Attache is essentially a place for the well-heeled and is popular with businessmen and yuppies amongst others. Open until 1am on Friday and Saturday night, otherwise midnight, L'Attache's radiant atmosphere makes it a pleasant place for a late evening drink.

THE LAST DROP
74-78 The Grassmarket

This pub has the cheerful historical connection of being located next to the spot where Edinburgh's public gallows once stood. To commemorate this, the owner has retained the original maroon exterior design which dates from the eighteenth century. The interior is suitably 'olde worlde' and homely but any ghosts from the gallows have been long swept away by the student clientele.

Only when Donald Mackinlay is fully satisfied will he give it his name.

Just as his father and his father before him have done.

Donald Mackinlay blends the whisky that bears his family name. Five generations of Mackinlay master blenders, 170 years of involvement in this unique blend that is the epitome of the traditional, original Scotch whisky.

Much has changed since those early years. The distinctive mellow five year old blend is now sold throughout the world. However, the principles of quality remain the same.

Only whisky reaching Donald Mackinlay's high standard is given his name.

After all, Donald has more than his own name to live up to.

The Original Mackinlay.

The true taste of traditional Scotch whisky.

THE ORIGINAL
MACKINLAY

CHARLES MACKINLAY & CO. LTD., 9-21 SALAMANDER PLACE, LEITH, EDINBURGH EH6 7JL. TEL. 031-554 4404 TELEX: 72624 WHISKY G. FAX: 031-554 1531

THE MALT SHOVEL
11-15 Cockburn Street
THE MALT SHOVEL TOO
(formerly Copper's)
19 Cockburn Street

These two combined are something of a beer drinker's paradise. Long established as one of Edinburgh's best real ale houses, The Malt Shovel is big and busy, decorated with assorted beer-making equipment. Speciality ales include Cameron's, Mitchell's, Theakstons', Malton's, Fuller's, Tetley's, the popular Maclay's and regular 'guest' beers. If you are not a beer connoisseur, there is a selection of lagers and ciders to keep you happy.

The food in here is good quality but reasonably priced, with a tempting salad bar and good home-made soup. All available from 12 noon-8pm Monday-Saturday. Perhaps due to the emphasis on quality beers, the bar tends to be popular with businessmen and 'serious' drinkers who want to be guaranteed a good pint. Packed at lunchtime and after work. Busiest night is Friday but also popular is Tuesday night when there is a regular jazz band, 'Swing', at 9pm. Malt Shovel Too is closed on Sundays.

OBLOMOV
top of the Mound
11/13 North Bank Street

This Dutch-style café/bar is named after a fictional Russian character who cannot get out of bed. A rather quirky decor consisting of carpeted tables, a poster-adorned ceiling and very odd lights add a slightly forced but laid-back atmosphere. The crowds tend to be image-conscious and trendy, having a pre-clubbing drink or two.

There are the usual beers and lagers on draught, including Stella and bottled continental beers. In the downstairs bar, a Friday night club has recently opened with small bands and cabaret style entertainment. The upstairs bar serves coffee and great tasting cakes all day with lunches from 12 noon-3pm. Look out for the beer garden due to open in the Festival.

ODDFELLOWS
14 Forrest Road

In its two years of existence, Oddfellows has established itself as THE student pub in Edinburgh. And there is plenty of room for them all, as the huge interior can hold as many as 350 people.

Oddfellows Hall itself has a history as varied and unusual as the numerous artefacts that dot the bar: bibles, stuffed animals, crockery, tall ships, model car, a Red Indian, to name a few. Originally, a boxing arena, it has been a dance hall, flea market, record exchange, Hare Krishna temple and home of the Oddfellows themselves, a charitable body.

An impressive, carved, stone facade stands above the narrow entrance. Go up the corridor inside and you will be confronted with the commanding spectacle of a large island bar surrounded by ample seating space, with a balcony circling the entire pub. Upstairs, at one end of the hall is an interesting painted design, featuring the coat-of-arms and standard of the Oddfellows.

Apart from the beers served on draught— Campbell's 70/- and 80/-, Murphy's Irish stout, Castle Eden ale—Oddfellows has a variety of bottled beers and lagers, as well as several of the 'trendier' canned lagers. The menu has recently undergone a price revision, with the cost of a meal actually coming down, and considerably too. Platters on offer range from baked potatoes (with a choice of several fillings) and burgers, to more adventurous meat and vegetarian dishes.

The pub is open until midnight during the week, and 2am at the weekend, (perhaps even 3am during the Festival). An added attraction is the recently re-introduced cocktail happy hour (5.30-7.00 Monday-Wednesday), offering half-price cocktails.

THE PELICAN
209 The Cowgate

The Pelican opened its doors for the first time early in 1989. In the previous six months, extensive refurbishment had transformed the former Gilded Balloon from a dark and somewhat dingy haunt into an expansive and chic pub and bistro. The large Gilded Balloon restaurant has become the pub area, complete with arty wall frieze, 'mezzanine', a mixture of benches and tables, and a small stage.

Like all pubs owned by Whitbread, The Pelican has on draught Stella, Heineken and Moosehead, as well as the usual beers; in fact the same stock as Oddfellows, another Whitbread pub. At the weekends it is usually comfortably busy, although it must be said that its desire to attract a City Cafe-type crowd (i.e. the young and stylish) has thus far failed somewhat, an indication that perhaps there are only so many cool folk in Edinburgh. However,

the appearance of bands, usually on a Thursday, has proved to be a popular attraction, particularly due to a selective choice of acts, ensuring a high standard of entertainment.

Another feature growing in popularity is the 'Spinning Wheel', a device whereby a light spins a wheel detailing a variety of reduced-price drinks: 'lager frenzy', 'get canned', 'slammerama', and 'vino splitto' among others. It does not take much to work out what the cheap drinks are there. All told, this has got to be one of the more 'interesting' ways of ordering your drink.

At the same time, the old bar has become a bistro. Here the tables are decked out in carpet fabric, and it is a tasteful setting in which to sample The Pelican's various gastronomic delights. The emphasis is on nouvelle cuisine—crepes, fish and chicken dishes—but more standard stuff is also available at a decent price. Best of all, the bistro is open until 5am on Fridays and Saturdays, serving breakfasts.

RUTHERFORD'S BAR
Drummond Street

It is unlikely that anyone could miss the impressive wooden frontage of this pub. Situated opposite Stewart's Bar and Woods, the barber, this little street has three institutions from the past.

Built just inside the old city wall in 1834,

its design remains unchanged. Both the bar and lounge are small. The upper beaten panelling which covers the back wall of the bar and the skylight are both features peculiar to it.

The atmosphere is of a working man's pub, and the clientele is made up mostly of regular drinkers who travel a well-worn path between here and the bookies round the corner in Nicholson Square.

STEWART'S BAR
Drummond Street

A wrought iron lampost serves as an original signpost outside this old pub.

Purchased in 1916 by Mr Stewart, who sold it 75 years later to the present owner, who himself has worked in the pub for the past 50 years, little has changed. Engraved on the frosted glass of a doorway are the words 'semper eaden' meaning: always the same.

There is a long bar and two rooms adjacent, a sitting room which houses a television, and a back room, which can be booked by anyone, free of charge, for any purpose.

The woodwork is very pleasing and the barrels over the bar are part of the decor.

Whisky is served in ¼ gill measures. Sandwiches are served, and mussels peddled at weekends.

This pub could be described as a father-son or even a family pub. The atmosphere here is one of friendliness and joviality.

Hours of opening: 11am-midnight Monday-Saturday, 12.30-2.30pm and 6.30-11pm Sundays.

THE TAP O'LAURISTON
80 Lauriston Place

The Tap O'Lauriston, situated on Lauriston Place across the road from the Art College, at first glance, appears to be one of Edinburgh's least promising pubs. Built into the corner of a large concrete building, its exterior is unaesthetic, but those who venture inside will find a pub with most of the qualities that go to create a good 'local'.

The Tap is made up of two adjoining areas separated by the bar. The smaller of the two is frequented largely by students from the Art College, while the other draws a more general local crowd. This larger area sports a TV and fruit machine along with the essential dart board, while the other houses a nice Juke Box. Decor throughout The Tap is fairly basic, with a few art posters perhaps for the benefit of the Art College students. The furnishings too are far from plush but are pleasantly comfortable and worn.

The fairly average range of draught beers includes cask-conditioned McEwan's 80/-, Murphy's Irish Stout and Beck's, and prices are very reasonable with change from £1 for most pints. The Tap also boasts lengthy opening hours: 1am on Thursday, Friday and Saturday, otherwise midnight.

The Tap O'Lauriston is a pleasant place to stop for a drink and is inexpensive. The atmosphere is always friendly, and at weekends it draws a lively crowd.

TRADER VIC'S

Trader Vic's is one of several new pubs which have appeared on Victoria Street and it is surely the best of the bunch. Some may remember this place in its 'Nicky Tams' days, though a complete transformation has occurred since then.

Trader Vic's is an atmospheric pub: when you venture through to the back you come upon a dark and intimate candlelit area ideal for a late night tête-à-tête. The decor is rather unusual. Numerous magazine photographs have been pasted to the walls to give a surprisingly tasteful effect. Trader Vic's also sports some rather interesting basketwork.

Though Trader Vic's is actually attached to The Mission nightclub below, it provides a very relaxed atmosphere—perhaps somewhere to escape from the noisy and energetic surroundings underneath. With its late opening hours, it comes highly recommended.

THE BLACK BULL
12 The Grassmarket

In common with several of the hostelries in the Grassmarket, The Black Bull has a considerable historical background stretching back to 1673 when it was an inn owned by John Smith, and adjoined to his blacksmith's business. While the horses may have gone, the pub does retain a traditional interior and the walls are festooned with paintings of old Edinburgh barometers, mirrors and the like.

The beers are of good quality and are supplemented by guest beers which are marked up on the blackboard above the bar. The range of bottled beers is wide including offerings from Japan and Jamaica. Unlike most other pubs, the Bull goes out of its way to provide a fairly extensive choice of wines, including champagne, and thereby challenges the resistance of most pubs in the city to stocking wines. Pies, meats, curries and salads are on offer between 12.00 and 2.30 for around £2.50.

All of these points go to make the Black Bull nearly always crowded, especially at the weekend. A word of warning before you try the toilets. 'Black Bulls' can be translated as Gents W.C., while 'Daisie Bells' denotes the room where noses can be powdered.

THE BLUE BLANKET
232 Canongate

The most notable thing about this pub is the stone mural on the front which depicts the scene at Jerusalem when the city was liberated in the 12th century by a band of Scots. Mind you, it might as well be a picture of the scene at opening time when the hordes of enthusiastic drinkers who love this place charge the door to get at the bar.

The interior is even less attractive than the exterior. The bar is big and over-crowding is rarely a problem. It is decorated with fake timbers and rafters. However, this old-world quaintness is completely at odds with the CD juke box and the fruit-machines.

PUB
FILLOSOPHY

" I LOOK AT IT
THIS WAY... "

BULL AND BUSH
81-83 Lothian Road

The interior of the Bull and Bush has been directly copied from that of the Black Bull in the Grassmarket: red seats, red walls and red ceilings, fancy cornices, etc. The effect is pretty offensive to look at, but this is still one of the most popular pubs on the Lothian Road.

The large open fire and pictures of silent movie stars give a little style to hyperbolic decor, while the availability of Warsteiner lager on draught and the lethal Diamond White cider in bottles are marks in its favour. Also notable is the Maclay's 80/- beer.

The Bull and Bush is situated close to the Filmhouse, Lyceum Theatre and Usher Hall, and just across the road from the Sheraton Hotel, and I cannot help but think that its popularity depends more on how handy it is for theatre-goers and hotel guests rather than on any inherent attraction.

THE BURNT POST
133 Lothian Road

The Burnt Post is a busy and well-known pub on the city's Lothian Road where it successfully competes with a veritable glut of public houses. Its popularity with visitors, as well as with Edinburgh residents, is borne out in healthy sales of Burnt Post T-shirts and sweatshirts, and in the return of familiar faces every year for rugby internationals and the like. At weekends this is a favourite stop for the happy hordes on their way to the Amphitheatre, Xanatec and Coasters discos nearby. A clean, thoroughly modern establishment, it is curiously decorated with antique sporting equipment and is regally overlooked by a giant moosehead affixed to one wall.

The draught beers are brewed by Alloa and they sell at average city-centre prices. Something of a rarity is the low-alcohol cider and wine. The house wine comes in both white and red, a choice you do not always find in an Alloa bar.

CANDLEMAKERS ARMS
2 Cowgatehead, Grassmarket

The Candlemakers Arms, tucked into one corner of the Grassmarket, is a small, friendly pub which prides itself on selling some of the least pricey beer in the area. Tennent's Lager, Export 80/-, and Tartan Special all sell for around £1.00, a figure which still seems to me the decent price for a pint. Unlike its flashier Grassmarket rivals, the Candlemakers is not heavily patronised by Edinburgh's student fraternity and relies instead on local regulars and those attracted by the live music which it stages.

The Candlemakers Arms is certainly an essential stop for lovers of folk music with Scottish and Irish folk music played to a busy house on Thursday, Friday and Saturday nights when the bar stays open until 1am in the summer.

Renovation work last year has improved the place a lot, smoothing out the rough edges and making the place more comfortable. Although somewhat quieter and more traditional than its near neighbours, it is also worth considering for a visit during a tour of the Grassmarket drinking dens, if only for the sake of your pocket.

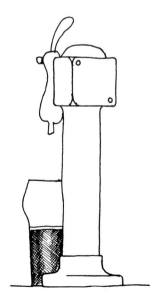

COVENANTERS
158 The High Street

While the name of this pub conjures up images of an establishment resplendent in material which remembers and portrays the signing of the Covenant in the 17th century, the reality is that Covenanters is more reminiscent of a modern hotel's lounge bar.

Plans are afoot to refurbish this bar before the summer, a change which was precipitated by the arrival of new management in October last year. However, at the time of writing, Covenanters was a compact and quiet bar which seems to be aimed at serving those in their late twenties and thirties who could, if I may be so bold, be described as young and somewhat upwardly mobile.

DEACON BRODIE'S TAVERN
435 Lawnmarket

Standing on the Royal Mile, only a moment's walk from the Castle and St Giles, Deacon Brodie's tavern is perfectly positioned to attract the thirsty tourist. In addition, it can also boast a ready-made history of its own which perhaps only Greyfriars Bobby can match.

The William Brodie, Deacon of the Incorporation of Wrights, to whom the establishment is dedicated, was a wealthy and respected citizen of eighteenth-century Edinburgh. In a double life despicable enough to inspire Robert Louis Stevenson's classic 'Dr Jekyll and Mr Hyde', he sunk to gambling and crime, carrying out robberies of great daring. Apprehended and brought to justice in 1788, Brodie was executed close to where the pub stands today. Shortly before his arrest, he had improved on the method of dispatching criminals by substituting a trap door for the ancient practice of the double ladder.

A lifesize figure of the unfortunate Deacon now sits beneath the stairway connecting the two bars of the Tavern, while the decor suitably invokes the atmosphere of old Edinburgh. In keeping with the main theme, paintings inside and out depict the story. Further historical

interest is provided by the antique ceiling in the lower bar, one of only two of its kind which survive.

Bought over by the Alloa Brewery Company two years ago, the pub has recently been renovated to its great improvement. In the elegant and comfortably furnished lounge bar upstairs, a selection of reasonably priced and well-presented meals are served all afternoon. The draught beers are of the usual Alloa variety, including Guinness and Lowenbrau Strong Lager, both less expensive than in some other Old Town pubs. The Englishman's favourite Tetley Bitter (£1.12) and draught L.A. are also on tap.

Deacon Brodie's is a large and busy pub, always lively in the evenings and often full to overflowing during the summer. Besides attracting throngs of tourists, it also serves as a popular meeting place for businessmen, students, lawyers, and all manner of Edinburgh residents. For a place of its size it is, however, remarkably quiet in one respect—the absence of loud music means the only din is that of conversation. Deacon Brodie's is one of Edinburgh's favourite watering holes. It should be one of yours.

ENSIGN EWART
521 Lawnmarket, Edinburgh EH1

Because of its situation on the doorstep of the Castle, the Ensign Ewart does a roaring trade with soldiers and tourists. The Ensign in question was a hero of the Scots' Greys at Waterloo who is buried in the Castle esplanade. Single-handed, he captured the standard of the famous French Invincibles which is now on display in the Castle museum. Portraits and battle scenes complementing the story adorn the walls of this small dimly-lit pub.

The customary Old Edinburgh feel is augmented by the low-beamed ceiling although it is something of a disappointment to find that the huge fireplace contains an electric fire.

The historical angle aside, the Ensign Ewart also attracts custom through its popular folk nights. A regular turnover of musicians can be heard on Tuesday, Thursday and Sunday evenings, and their recorded work can be purchased on the spot.

You will not pay much over the odds for a drink in what might potentially be something of a tourist trap. Guinness, Lowenbrau, Dryborough's Heavy and the usual Alloa beers are all reasonably priced for this part of town. Lunch available from 12.00-3.00 and pies on offer throughout the evening.

Somewhat off the beaten track for Edinburgh's resident weekend drinkers, with the obvious exception of the folk enthusiasts, the Ensign Ewart is a cosy traditional pub which is well worth a visit.

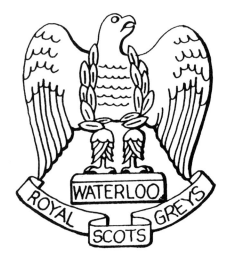

FIDDLERS ARMS
9/11 Grassmarket

The Fiddlers Arms has somehow avoided becoming prey to hordes of under-25s, unlike most of the pubs in the Grassmarket. Instead it has retained its individual character by providing good ales and not building a restaurant or a bistro and thereby alienating some of the regulars.

The pub itself is quite small with very little sitting room, but the appeal of a place like this lies in standing at the bar chatting to the bar-staff and locals. In the downstairs area the pool table and the low beer prices attracts a much younger crowd.

GREYFRIARS BOBBY
34 Candlemaker Row

The legend of Greyfriars Bobby has always been attractive to tourists in Edinburgh, partly because of the 'Wonderful World of Disney' presentation of the tale. As a result a well-worn trail is made by camera-laden visitors to Greyfriars Churchyard where the faithful canine, Bobby, kept watch over his master's grave, and also to the statue of the aforementioned dog which is found on George IV Bridge.

Sandwiched neatly between these fringe attractions is Greyfriars Bar, one of Edinburgh's best known and popular pubs. It too is steeped in history and the building itself dates back to the 1720s when it was made up of a number of shops and a blacksmiths. The present arrangement has managed to retain the old-style exterior including the distinctive leaded windows which run the length of the pub.

The inside of the pub is in the old Edinburgh style with pictures, drawings, plaques, etc. Though the pub is spacious there are few seats because it is so narrow. This is especially irksome at lunchtime when the crowds are attracted by the high-quality meals that are on offer.

Apart from the tourists, the pub is popular amongst the students from the Law and Architecture faculties of the University. This is especially true late at night when the atmosphere become heady with alcoholic excess. (Opening times: 11.30-1am Tuesday-Friday, till 2am on Saturday).

THE HALFWAY HOUSE
24 Fleshmarket Close

It is not exactly difficult to see how this place comes by its name. It is a welcome haven for a rest on the way up Fleshmarket Close between getting off the train at Waverley Station and the long trek home. Going in the other direction, it is a good base to visit the Fruitmarket and City Art Galleries on Market Street.

By any standard, this is a small pub and one can imagine it being a cramped gin-house in medieval Edinburgh. Due to its size, the drinks selection is understandably restricted but with moderate prices and 80/- on tap you should have few complaints.

The regulars, mainly workmen, shift workers and hacks from the neighbouring *Scotsman* office are, in general, friendly and good natured and provide an opportunity to meet real Edinburgh people.

JENNY HA'S BAR
65 Canongate, 1 Brown's Close

Jenny Ha's is positioned within easy walking distance of most of the sights on the lower part of the Royal Mile with Holyrood Palace being particularly close. Set slightly off the road, but still very much part of the High Street bustle, it's ideal for either a quiet afternoon tipple or a friendly evening drink.

It is not the kind of pub to stock an array of imported bottle lagers, but the draft ale and export is more welcomed by the largely middle-aged regulars. The staff are cheerful and friendly without ever being intrusive and serve reasonably-priced lunches between twelve and two during most of the year, with the possibility of longer meal times over the summer.

THE JOLLY JUDGE
7a James Court

A keen eye is required if you are to spot the Jolly Judge which is hidden away up James Court, off the Lawnmarket. The search, however, is more than worthwhile. As with the other public houses in the vicinity of the Castle, history and tradition are heavily stressed in the design and atmosphere.

Although the Jolly Judge has only been in operation for nine years, the building itself is reckoned to be of 13th century construction, the same age as the middle part of the Castle. The low ceiling is built from old ship timbers taken from a Leith cargo vessel, and is decorated in keeping with the style which would have adorned the ship's interior. A large, real fire and soft lighting help create an intimate atmosphere which is never broken by loud music.

Burton's 90/- and a reasonably-priced pint of Guinness are offered amongst the draught beers, whilst the Jolly Judge provides a wider choice of wines than you will find in most pubs. A notable selection of malt whiskies is also displayed, doubtless to the great interest of tourists and locals alike. Bar lunches, mainly salads, are sold in the afternoons with filled rolls available all day.

The Jolly Judge is fortunate in having the use of James Court as a makeshift beer garden. Though hardly a garden in the strictest sense of the word, it is nonetheless rather pleasant to sit out here during the summer. A few more tables and chairs outside would not, however, go amiss. Its proximity to the Sheriff Court, from whence the name is derived, sees it fill up with lawyers in the early evenings. Judges, jolly or otherwise, are at a premium, but you may spot an advocate or two. Expatriate Americans also tend to congregate here, stateside accents are in evidence all the year round.

This is certainly one of the better of the snug, old-fashioned pubs which cluster along the Royal Mile. In its limited confines, you may be hard pressed to find a seat in the evenings, but this should not adversely affect your final verdict.

THE KASBAR
71 Cowgate

Anyone who has already visited The Kasbar will tell you it is much more than a pub, more an experience. Very rarely will anyone admit being there in a less than intoxicated state. It is a haven for serious drinkers of all ages and background.

Situated in the Cowgate, within easy stumbling distance from the earlier-closing Grassmarket and High Street pubs, the Kasbar is undeniably the perfect ending to even the most unperfect evening. Two bars and plenty of seating more than make up for the primitive toilets and lack of civilisation.

NEGOTIANTS
45/47 Lothian Street

There are few pubs in Edinburgh where a request for raspberry lager would be met with anything other than a derogatory look. No such problems, however, in Negotiants where the range of imported lagers is enough to satisfy even the most adventurous drinker. The price, of course, is a drawback with the imported bottles starting at about £2.00.

Its location means that it is a very popular place during the Festival. The upstairs bar has waitress service and a formal atmosphere while downstairs is much more of a free-for-all and consequently much livelier. Live bands are also a regular attraction helping to lift the gloomy darkness.

THE POSEUR

THE PRESERVATION HALL
9 Victoria Street

At the Preservation Hall, the accent is firmly on live entertainment with blues and jazz bands doing their thing every night of the week. Admission is usually free, although you may be charged a pound or two to see popular Edinburgh acts such as Avalon or Tam White at weekends. On such evenings, you will not however be required to drink up until around 1am. A busy night can see a sizeable crowd jammed in to hear the bands, and on boisterous summer evenings it can get stiflingly hot. Not that you would be fooled into thinking you were in New Orleans. The large portrait of a kilted piper which overlooks the small stage rather gives the game away.

As might be expected, the 'Pres' is not exactly sumptuous, rough charm is perhaps the best description. Recent redecoration has seen the place plump for deep burgundy in a big way, though the quotations and proverbs daubed around the walls remain an amusing distraction. Comfortable seating, indeed seating in general, is rather lacking and the toilets could be of a higher standard.

Fortunately there are no such problems with regard to the drinks. The large, circular bar offers a wide choice of draught beers and it is well worth splashing out on the excellent Holstein lager or the Murphy's Irish Stout. Healthily sized and highly appetizing pizzas are sold all day.

Previously the venue for the Edinburgh Jazz Festival, the Preservation Hall with this August host a special week of blues n' boogie during which the joint will doubtless be jumping in time-honoured fashion. Suffice to say, this is not the place for a quiet, intimate evening. But then who wants a quiet chat on a Saturday night?

WHITE HART INN
34 Grassmarket

The White Hart Inn is probably one of the less well known pubs in the Grassmarket area. Yet behind this relative obscurity lies the claim that it is the oldest inn in Edinburgh. While dates supporting this are rather hazy, the Inn does nevertheless have a proud heritage. Robert Burns stayed there during 1791, during which time he is said to have composed 'Ae Fond Kiss', and twelve years later, his English counterpart, William Wordsworth, stopped over with his sister Dorothy.

The present pub is one of the few remaining in Edinburgh which still has a hanging sign outside. Beyond this the pub is fairly 'rough and ready', its decor being fairly basic and coarse. However, it is a pub which is popular with natives of Edinburgh who are attracted less by plush furnishings than the live music every night in unpretentious surroundings.

Beyond the live musical offerings, the White Hart Inn has the usual pub fare, though its bar snacks go further than toasted sandwiches offering gammon steaks, veal and so on for around £2.00. It offers four to five beers on draught with a pint costing about £1 on average.

THE WORLD'S END
4 The High Street

The world came to a grisly end for Sir James Stanfield in 1687 when he was murdered on this site. Investigations revealed that when his son touched the corpse it bled and he was subsequently found guilty of the murder.

Gruesome details aside, the World's End is a busy pub because of its location on the corner of St Mary's Street and the High Street. The nooks and cornices of the bar itself mean that there's always a quiet, more intimate corner to be found away from the bustle of the main pub. There are very few outstanding features with the usual selection of beers and a laid-back atmosphere, except when the live singers come on late at night.

INTRODUCTION TO THE NEW TOWN

Even when it was built, the planners of the New Town understood what a different place it would be to Edinburgh's Old Town. Maybe it was the closely built, cramped, dirty and disorganized buildings which clung to the hill between the Castle and the Palace which inspired James Craig, the designer of the first New town, to plan the wide sunny boulevards and symmetrical squares which characterize early drawings of George Street, Charlotte Square and St Andrew's Square.

The elegant Georgian buildings, which became an alternative to the tenements of the Old Town after North Bridge was built, set the tone for the New Town. Although Princes Street is a bit of a nightmare these days, a couple of minutes' walk takes you to the tranquil places of the Moray estate and the wide streets of the West End where the feeling of light and space is always apparent.

The uniform grandeur of these buildings hides the large variety of residents who live in the New Town. Many of the apartments remain as large and luxurious as they were designed to be but many of them were never very grand, housing servants and the middle classes who worked in the shops and small businesses of the area. Other flats have been broken up so large numbers of people can cram into one residency.

The pubs of the New Town were not accommodated into the original architectural plans. On the whole they are found in basements and behind the bigger blocks of flats. But this gives them an underground quality which a landlord can use to great effect. The taverns of Rose Street are quite a different matter and nothing short of experience can adequately give the feeling of that place late in a Friday night.

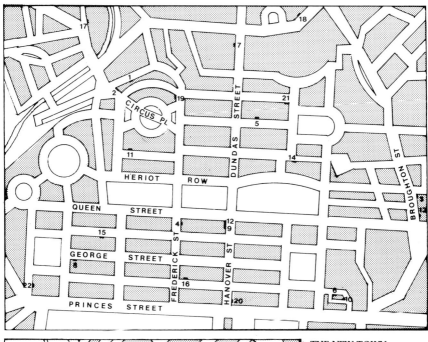

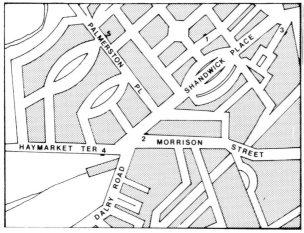

THE NEW TOWN

1. The Antiquary
2. The Baillie
3. The Barony
4. Café Biarritz
5. The Claret Jug
6. The Café Royal
7. Clark's Bar
8. Consort Cocktail Bar
9. Edinburgh Wine Bar
10. The Guildford Arms
11. Kay's
12. The Mary Rose
13. Mather's
14. The Northumberland Bar
15. Oxford Bar
16. Rose Street Brewery
17. Shambles
18. Smithies Ale House
19. The St Vincent
20. Three Tuns
21. Tilted Wig
22. Whigham's

WEST END

1. The Auld Hoose
2. Haymarket Bar
3. Platform One
4. Ryrie's
5. West End Hotel

THE ANTIQUARY
72-76 St Stephen Street

Embedded in a strip of a St Stephen Street basement, the Antiquary does not exactly publicise its existence with neon lights, but demonstrates a genuine popularity in its stream of customers. In many ways, it is a pub that manages to defy conventional categories. Housing as many Sloanes during the week as the Tilted Wig, it also serves a fair quantity of Edinburgh's bohemia and appears to be similarly at home with the local bikers.

The atmosphere is generally laid back and unimpaired by the all-too-frequent cluster of drinkers in other pubs that fix their eyes on the door to see which groupies are going to make their next entrance. Music has a relatively limited menu, mainly going in for Level 42 and Bryan Adams. However, musicians are frequently invited to the pub to play and on some nights they have jamming sessions, with the floor open to anyone who wants to try their hand. The barmen are convivial and efficient and seem to be more knowledgeable than usual about the drinks they are serving: Tetley's, Burton's and Furstenberg on tap.

Altogether, a pub worth frequenting, if only for the Bloody Marys—the best anywhere in Edinburgh.

THE BAILLIE BAR
2 St Stephen Street

Situated below street level on the corner of St Stephen Street and North-West Circus Place, it is easy to miss the Baillie. But any pub with an ancient 'Guinness Is Good For You' sign outside cannot be bad news.

The Baillie swarms with yuppies at lunch times. The food is imaginative and well-cooked and served in a cosy little adjoining dining room. This room is ideal to invade if you come in a large group later in the evening, but does tend to fill with smoke.

The main room is dominated by the impressive floating bar. Service is friendly but you can wait a while for your pint on a busy weekend evening. There is a warming 'village local' feeling to the Baillie—probably due to the total absence of juke boxes, fruit machines and video games.

Perhaps because it is practically subterranean you can conveniently forget that it is pouring with rain outside. Either way, this is a pub where you are assured of a decent cask-conditioned pint and a lively atmosphere. Baillie means a judge in Scots, but there were not many sober examples of those by the time I left.

THE BARONY BAR
81/83 Broughton Street

Designed in 1898, The Barony is situated in the ancient Baronial Burgh of Broughton, a place notorious as a haunt of witches. The street was built on the site of some old thatched cottages, one of which was popularly known as the 'Witches Howff', and the cellars of Old Broughton Street were originally the dungeons of the Tolbooth, in which the followers of the 'Black Arts' were incarcerated while awaiting execution.

In more recent years it has become the night-time haunt of the New Town Sloanes: in term-time the convivial spirit is somewhat dominated by their presence. Expect to rub shoulders not only with the Reverend from 'Take The High Road', but with a multitude of ethnic prints, peroxide blondes, and big, smug cliques indulging in much kissing of cheeks. The more they imbibe the louder they get, so beware if your ears are sensitive to a Home Countries drawl.

Outside, a coven of casuals has been known to congregate, apparently without menace; the bar is also plagued by the ubiquitous fruit machine and juke box, which seems out of character when you consider that the Barony provides free live jazz twice weekly. These sessions enhance the dynamic atmosphere of the bar, but avoid them if you are given to contemplative thought over a quiet pint—they are noisy, smoky and packed.

This comfortable, busy bar offers waitress service and a fairly wide lunch menu, including a vegetarian selection: average price of a substantial meal is £2.70. The beers on tap include Beck's, Murphy's and cask-conditioned 80/-, with a very small selection of bottled beers, a broad spectrum of wines, and adequate provision of alcohol-free drinks. Freshly-squeezed orange juice is available on request.

The interior of the Barony has been preserved in its original state, with an ornate teak frontage, hand-painted tiles and a rough-hewn wooden floor. It can

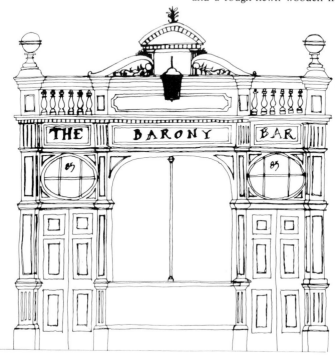

seat about 50 people around polished bottles of various sizes—a functional and pleasant change from the copper-topped uniformity of so many public houses. There is plenty of space for the flitting of the proverbial social butterfly, and benches outside for those hardy enough to brave the temperamental Scottish weather.

If this has enticed you to visit, perhaps I will see you there, because I am off to the Barony for a pint, a packet of pistachio nuts and an eavesdrop on loud anecdotes of exotic foreign travel.

CAFÉ BIARRITZ
61 Frederick Street

Masquerading in an art deco style and clearly inspired by the McDonald's Hamburger School of Design, this upwardly aspiring wine bar caters only for the over 21s and ends up attracting an eclectic clientele from aspiring yuppies to the more local regulars.

Serving cocktails as well as most of the regular beers, prices tend on the steep side of reasonable, and the food is adequate. The big attraction is the jazz on Friday night. Otherwise it is quiet enough to have an intimate tête-à-tête, without having to scream over the conversation of others.

Overall, the Café Biarritz adequately fulfils its function of providing a comfortable place to quench thirst in a civilised environment.

CAFÉ NOIR
Waverley Market
Waverley Bridge

While plans to pedestrianize Princes Street get no further than the council's drawing-board, the centre of Edinburgh's main shopping area becomes increasingly manic and sweaty. It is, however, possible to escape the mayhem at Café Noir in the new shopping mall at the Waverley Market.

The Café Noir is a small bistro and bar on the ground level of the market. There is a small restaurant serving French-style food as well as the main bar. There is a large and trendy selection of beers on tap including Stella, Heineken, Moosehead, Strongbow, Campbell's 70/-, Guinness and Murphy's Irish Stout. Restaurant prices range from 95p for a hot croissant to £6.50 for grilled sword-fish and black-pepper sauce.

CAFÉ ROYAL
17 West Register Street

The Café Royal was first opened in 1826 when the interior was based on the style of the Second French Empire. In 1898 it was acquired by Charles Clark, who also owned the Royal British Hotel. He closed down the hotel side of the business and instructed the barman to send customers to his other premises.

The Café Royal's opulent ground-floor bars, classics of the *fin de siecle* interior decoration, were put in by Clark and are still in superb condition. An impressive feature of both bars are the Doulton Lambeth Faience tiled murals, the marbled walls and the ornate ceiling which are redolent of the middle-class prosperity and confidence at the end of Queen Victoria's reign.

The 'period' interior of this pub belies its distinctly professional clientele. Everywhere you look, credit cards and company accounts sustain the bulk of the regulars who pour out of nearby offices.

The recent shift towards 'designer' beer labels conceals the well-to-do loutishness of the lager drinkers. For those who are particular about the architecture around them, and remain sentient enough to enjoy it, the Café Royal bar is a gem in the quivering navel of Edinburgh night life where one might well be arrested by the intention to loiter. Certainly a haunt for those seeking solace from sobriety, the more temperate will find its slightly impersonal size an invitation to self-consciousness.

CLARK'S BAR
142 Dundas Street

The rather plain facade hides a friendly but basic pub with two snugs at the back of the premises. It is a working man's place but there were complaints that yuppies were creeping in. Unless you are heard making crass comments about football you are left alone to enjoy the perfect beer, if not the dressed down interior.

The bar staff are efficient, but not enthusiastic. This comes as a welcome change from the normal policy where someone wipes around you every five minutes and takes all your empties away so you do not know how drunk you are. The barman's answer to my asking if they had a backgammon board succinctly sums up the place, 'you're here to drink, not play games'.

THE CLARET JUG
Howard Hotel
34 Great King Street

This pub is hidden in the basement of the Howard Hotel and from the outside there is practically no indication that it exists at all. Despite this, young people from the New Town frequent this pub in great numbers and it is especially popular amongst English students who flock to Edinburgh to attend University.

The pub can be very full just before supper-time when people go there to pop in for a quick one to set them up for the night, and on Sunday when the licence permits all day opening, when a lot of other pubs are shut. Vast red leather armchairs make this a very comfortable place to drink your pint.

Prices are average and a commendable pint of Websters may be obtained from the occasionally austere bar staff. A perfectly adequate lunch can be had for three or four pounds to provide Sunday or weekday blotting paper. In the summer, a few punters will mingle in the basement area outside. This pub does tend to fill up with ex-public schoolboys and the jolly hockey sticks brigades, but if that's your cup of tea, it's perfect. It gets crowded when Internationals are on, but then so does everywhere else.

CONSORT COCKTAIL BAR
The Roxburgh Hotel
38 Charlotte Square

The perfect retreat for the weary business-man or culture-blitzed tourist, the velvet-upholstered interior of the Consort bar is reminiscent of theatre bars and hotel lounges everywhere: comfortable, inoffensive and characterless. The combination of impersonal surroundings, hushed atmosphere and courteous, extremely professional bar staff, evidently appeals to those seeking a quiet drink—although is also a varied and above average menu, with correspondingly high prices.

The range of cocktails is impressive, catering for both the grey-suited men at the bar hunched over their *Financial Times,* and for the ever present table of subdued secretaries sipping brightly coloured drinks, submerged beneath cocktail umbrellas and glace cherries. The wine list is enticingly large, but the least expensive bottle is the house wine at £7 which suggests that the clientele tends to be of the credit card and expense account variety, especially during the Edinburgh Festival when the bar becomes the haunt of visiting journalists in need of a reviving dry martini.

EDINBURGH WINE BAR
110 Hanover Street

At lunchtime, this wine bar—furnished in country pub-style floral chintz and dark wood—is awash with Marks and Spencer carrier bags and leather briefcases, but in the evenings the average age of the clientele drops by a decade or two and the serious drinking begins.

The home-made soups, simple food and fresh salads are presumably the attraction during the day, as the wine list can only have a strong appeal for those with an unlimited capacity for Rioja. There are a couple of more expensive bottles—Chablis at £9.40, for example—but the average price is £6.50, which may explain why so many students use the place as their local pub. They usually overcome the problem of a shortage of tables by installing themselves on the staircase—an interesting practice that probably accounts for the younger age-range amongst the late night drinkers. You have to be agile to negotiate the leather jackets and pint mugs on your way up to the bar.

THE GUILDFORD ARMS
1 West Register Street

Situated next door to the posher Cafe Royal, just behind the statue of the Duke of Wellington, at the east end of Princes Street, the Guildford was established as a pub in 1896 by Mr James Dodds. In 1970, the ornate island counter was replaced by a bar set against the back wall, but apart from this one alteration the Guildford remains in the same state in which its original owner intended it to be.

Although generally fairly busy, you can usually escape the noise and bustle of the bar area by heading for one of the secluded little niches towards the back, and try to budge the pub cat from one of the seats.

A generous range of beers is available, with the full Belhaven and Tennent selections supplemented by Caledonian 80/-, the rare Harveston real ale, and the Scrumpy Jack cider.

The clientele is similar to any other pub in the centre of town, though at the weekend, conversation tends to be dominated by the football and racing

results. The only other hazard is the revolving door. Easily enough negotiated at the beginning of the evening, six pints later it represents an insurmountable obstacle. I struggled for ten minutes trying to escape once, before giving up and going back inside for another drink.

KAY'S BAR
39 Jamaica Street
off India Street

This wee boozer started out life in 1815 as an off licence, and to this day retains an old-fashioned atmosphere, the walls being lined with antique casks. Although a rather small pub, with an even smaller back room, it is rare to feel cramped.

Dave Mackenzie is a capable landlord who knows how to keep his real ales in fine condition. All the bar staff are extremely efficient and friendly. The selection of whisky is enormous and can keep you amused for hours. Ask Dave for one of his special brandies—£5 a shot. Open all day, lunches here are good value and there are usually a couple of traditional Scottish dishes to be had.

The atmosphere is easy-going so it is impossible to get out of the door without talking to someone. In winter, the pub is especially attractive due to the open fire at the end of the bar.

L'ODEON

L'Odeon, recently opened on George IVth Bridge, is, as its name suggests, a continental Bar/Café aimed, unashamedly, at those who hanker after a touch of the Parisian life. Like so many of the new breed of British bars, it veers away from the traditional pub atmosphere by creating a more up-market image using Art Nouveau styling adorned with a hotch-potch of French posters, signs and paraphernalia. Though such interiors are becoming some-what clichéd, L'Odeon manages to attain a degree of Gallic authenticity which makes it an unusual and pleasant haven any time of day. The newspaper rack would look perfectly comfortable harbouring copies of *Le Figaro* or *Le Monde,* and most of the

GOING TO THE PUB ?

clientele would look similarly comfortable reading them—instead the *Independent* with a jug of coffee, or a pint of lager is the norm.

From breakfast onwards there is very toothsome and reasonably priced food on offer, with the emphasis on crêpes and devilishly tempting puddings (the Alabama soft rock pie is a real treat) plus French cuisine on an ever-changing menu. Though many of the tables are so small it feels like eating off a postage stamp, L'Odeon generally feels quite roomy.

The bar itself offers Stella Artois as its main draught, though the usual Heavy, Heineken and supporting cast provide ample choice. There is also a good selection of wines in the £5-£6 a bottle range, which are served in stylish glasses by the genial bar-staff.

L'Odeon is a relaxed, stylish and civilised place to sit, drink and eat on an evening out, or if just passing. It is not a place to find yourself under the table, even if the tables allow it, but neither is it staid or boring. Sitting conveniently between Edinburgh University and Edinburgh offices, it should become increasingly popular.

THE MARY ROSE BISTRO
112 Hanover Street

On most evenings the 'Rose is crowded, noisy and ugly. Its late opening, until 2.30am most nights, has had a tendency to turn Hanover Street into Hangover Street for me on more than one occasion. On sober reflection, however, the late licence is about all it has going for it.

It was recently redecorated with movie star portraits which has made the interior look a bit like a pizza parlour. There are regular beers, Carlsberg, Castlemaine, McEwan's 80 shilling, Tartan, Murphy's etc, as well as continental bottled brands.

The attempts to attract the young affluent set are reflected by the wide range of food available. On my visit they seemed to be pushing a cocktail called Tropical Frog, consisting of vodka, blue bols, apricot liqueur and orange juice. If that doesn't make you throw up, there is always the intrusive conversation of the young gun clientele, arguing the relative merits of a Porsche vis-à-vis a GTI. After midnight, the yuppie element does definitely dominate.

Should you be understandably tempted towards a little creative mayhem, be warned. The bar walls are covered with intimidating admonitions promising dire punishment should you have the temerity to spill beer or drop rubbish on the floor.

One further irritation is the hard selling of pizzas that takes place towards closing time when customers' discernment tends to be clouded by that eighth pint. All things considered, an unfriendly elitist atmosphere makes this one place where I can thoroughly recommend the alternative of an early night. The 80/- always appears to be unusually cold, and is served in plastic glasses.

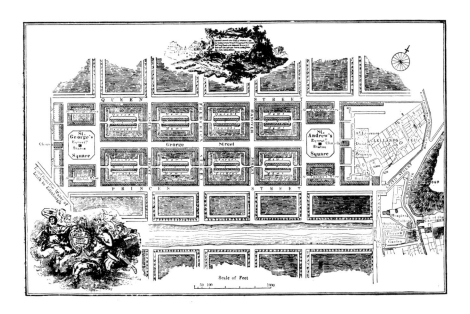

MATHERS
25 Broughton Street

Mathers pub is situated at the top of Broughton Street, a stone's throw from the Playhouse Theatre, and only five minutes walk from the East End of Princes Street. Even on my first visit there I realised it was a veritable gem of a pub standing far and above the mainstream, and in my humble opinion, an hour (or more!) spent within such a congenial watering hole should prove pleasurable to seasonal pubgoers and mad-buck hedonists alike.

On first entering one is immediately struck by the relaxed strains of conversation, so often unheard in contemporary public houses where the aspiring raconteur has not only to cope with their listeners' foibles but has to contend also with the aural intrusions of an ear-splitting juke box. The absence of this musical tyranny was indeed refreshing, as was that of the ubiquitous fruit machine.

The interior is moderately large with seating for about seventy and adequate standing space around the bar. There are two levels in the place, the upper being reached by four steps, which should present no problem to the average inebriate. Both levels boast an open hearth which add intimacy to what is otherwise an open bar. The clientele were a mixed bag of people ranging from students to business-men.

For the real ale drinker, Theakstons' Old Peculiar should excite even the most experienced palate. Although at £1.32 a pint, Old Peculiar does not come cheap, it is smooth, eminently drinkable and has a kick like a mule. Other beers on tap, Murphy's, Guinness, Special etc. average out about £1.05. There is a small selection of bottled beers but (also for the wine imbiber), there was only a house wine on offer. However, why drink wine when you can drink whisky and Mathers provides a wide selection of good malts.

So, if anyone bewails the demise of conversation, get down to Mathers, have a pint, and don't talk to the fierce looking elk on the wall because it won't talk back!

THE NORTHUMBERLAND BAR
1 Northumberland Place

There's no doubt about one thing, this is a quiet place to have a drink. Hidden in the mews below Abercromby Place, only those who already know about it are ever likely to find it. The beers on offer are Alloa. They are stored in a cellar with a dangerous reputation. The manager told me that a skull had been found there some years ago. A curse had clearly been attached to it because every time it had been moved, a disaster afflicted the pub.

THE OXFORD BAR
8 Young Street

In the dim and not so distant past, the Oxford Bar was generally acclaimed as a 'traditional' establishment where its proprietor, Willie Ross, made sure that women and Englishmen were refused service. Of course, if a place refused to serve Irish or Asians they would be rightly condemned as racist, but apparently women and the English were deserving victims.

Those days are thankfully gone, and this small quiet pub offers a welcome to all. Situated towards the West End, in Young Street, it manages to retain the feel of a friendly backstreet local. In fact the place could be out of the thirties, with a small bar area, and an unpretentious backroom decorated with whimsical pictures.

The choice of beers is as unremarkable as the decor. Tennent's 70/- and lager are supplemented by Caledonian and McEwan's 80/-, Younger's Heavy and Murphy's. The clientele is younger than might be expected, with the occasional West End businessman enjoying a quiet pint. 'Quiet' is probably the operative word at the Oxford. The clatter of dominoes usually presents a greater threat to the peaceful atmosphere than any raucous music. Altogether, an oasis of calm away from the wine-bar crowd.

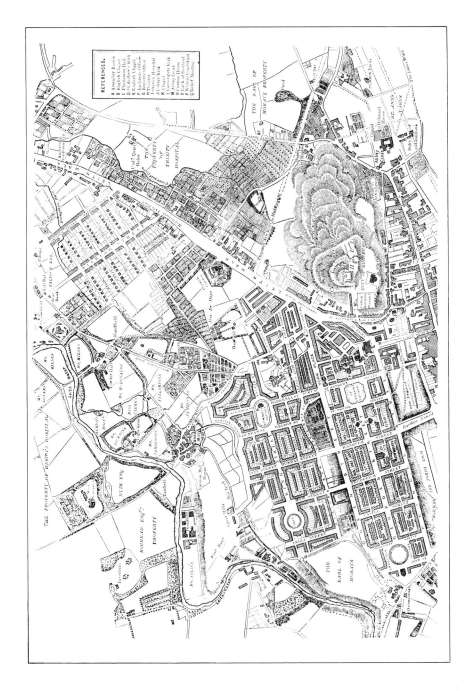

THE ROSE STREET BREWERY
55 Rose Street

The Rose Street Brewery deserves its reputation as one of Edinburgh's most unusual pubs. Firstly, it is Scotland's only mainland home-brew pub having been set up by Alloa Brewery in 1983, in the former White Cockade. The malt-extraction plant is unusually situated at the rear of the lounge bar and the vessels are visible through glass windows.

Secondly, it has the rare distinction of being a Rose Street pub that is worth a visit. Quiet at lunch times, the Brewery is usually packed in the evenings, though the plusher lounge bar upstairs is always worth a try. Downstairs, it is spacious, basic and attractively dingy. It is a hearty sort of place with live music on Tuesday and Thursday evenings, and a Sixties disco for 'ageing hippies' on Wednesdays. A dubious attraction is a seedy juke box with over 2,500 selections.

Like Diggers and the Fiddler's Arms, the real attraction of this pub is for the beer connoisseur. Auld Reekie 80/- is an excellent pint, brewed upstairs. Chalked up on a small blackboard in the pub is the Original Gravity of the latest brew, together with a mark awarded by the panel of tasters which includes Mr Borjucki, the charismatic Masterbrewer. Try the 90/- (O.G. 1056) — a wickedly creamy brew. Not recommended for lunchtime.

All in all, this is a pub with character where you do get service with a smile and a doorman on Friday and Saturday nights should mean that it never gets rough.

THE SHAMBLES
47 Deanhaugh

The Shambles takes its name from the medieval street in York so possibly the paintings on its facade of Robin Hood and Friar Tuck are a bit incongruous. Ye Olde theme is continued inside with an ingenious interior designed to mimic the York Street in miniature; as a result, one sits in little rooms of the little house of the little street, decorated with timber cladding and plates inexplicably nailed to the walls. In such a Toytown scenario, our more cynical readers may be expecting a big-eared barman to offer soda pop and lashings of ginger beer, but in fact the pub, for all its twee decoration, is remarkably charming, and the small rooms provide a privacy that few pubs can match.

The alcohol is directed more towards the lager drinker, with three types on tap, including Lowenbrau, and there is also a carry-out service of wines, beers and spirits. The Shambles has a pool table, a juke box and for lunch, Mrs Freely, the manager, provides students, pensioners and UB40 holders with an excellent 2-course lunch for only £1.80.

SMITHIES ALE HOUSE
47/51 Eyre Place

Smithies is a small pub with a thrust bar that takes up most of the inside. It is comfortable, carpeted and mirrored all around, which gives the effect of the pub being larger and lighter than it really is. There is a full lunch menu with everything being cooked on the premises and not just brought in and heated up.

On rugby International days, there are free stovies provided and although this is not the only reason to patronise this pub, it does show that they are friendly and eager to help. CAMRA's No 1 beer, Tetleys', makes a welcome appearance on the bar and there are a number of diverse whiskys and whiskeys. There is a pub football team which always seems to need players and a welcome absence of fruit machines and other distractions.

THE ST VINCENT
9 St Vincent Street

For several years the St Vincent had a temporary name of Coconut Tams, but following a facelift it has reverted to its former title. One of many basement bars at the bottom of the New Town, the St Vincent attracts a loyal band of regulars, but unlike many such Edinburgh pubs, a stranger will not open the door to encounter a barrage of acidic stares. Instead, the pub is always lively, often crowded (especially around 10pm) and has a wonderfully friendly array of bar staff who will provide you with cribbage, Trivial Pursuit and dominoes on request.

The St Vincent is nearly a hundred years old and still maintains a Victorian warmth in its decoration and furniture. There is a good range of beers, including a 'guest beer' (try Timothy Taylor's if they have it in) as well as an extensive range of whiskies. The alcoholic armoury is further strengthened by a very fine selection of wines which are available by the glass or bottle. A 3-course lunch is available as well as snacks throughout the day.

However, despite its considerable charm, the St Vincent, like other downstairs pubs will cause quite serious problems for anyone in a wheelchair—it may be advisable to telephone before arriving to check that someone will be able to help you get in.

THE THREE TUNS
7-11 Hanover Street

It is no accident that The Three Tuns is wedged between Miss Selfridge and Pizzaland. The character of this pub is dictated by considerations of mass marketing. The bare brick interior conjures up images of amicable evenings in warmer climates, but it fails to attract all but the most ephemeral visitors, and thus is disposed to the convenience of its customers rather than nurturing the prejudices of a distinct clientele. A jazz duo entertain spasmodically to an unresponsive audience at least one night a week. Err at your peril—only if forcibly evicted from all other establishments and utterly disenchanted with the other delights on offer in the surrounding area.

THE TILTED WIG
1-3 Cumberland Street

On the corner of Cumberland and Dundonald Streets, this establishment is run by its owner, Paddy Crossan, formerly of the original Paddy's Bar in Rose Street, in the days when people drank. The interior is not desperately attractive—a black and white checked linoleum floor with wallpaper specially ordered from France on the ceiling. But then you should be looking at your glass and not at the floor.

The clientele range from Old Etonian ra-ra students to retired couples and, of course, a large number of New Town lawyers. The dining room at the back may be hired for functions and also boasts a log fire.

The main bar and seating area is always neat and clean and one can order a modestly priced lunch until about 2pm. It usually closes in the afternoon except on Saturdays. In the summer, the grassy garden is a popular attraction. There are not many places in the New Town where one can drink outside. Cribbage, backgammon and the Landlord provide further entertainment.

WHIGHAMS WINE CELLARS
13 Hope Street

Easy to miss, Whighams is a converted wine cellar with a flagged and sawdust floor and a series of arched alcoves. Whighams is one of the few good wine bars in Edinburgh, and has gathered a faithful following, although the average night-time crowd seem to be attracted more by the atmosphere than by the excellent wine list.

The house wines are good value—especially if bought by the bottle rather than the glass. The rest of the list has been carefully selected, is reasonably priced and on the whole, less flashy than some of the Whighams regulars.

The bar provides a convenient resting place for filofaxes on weekday evenings, when the Edinburgh business community descends en masse—an influx that can make the already cramped wine cellars seem claustrophobic—but at weekends, the atmosphere is less frantic and the stone-walled alcoves tend to be occupied by ex-Fettesians lending support to their friends working behind the bar.

THE AULD HOOSE
27 William Street

William Street is one of the lesser known streets in Edinburgh although it does not deserve to be. Away from the uninspiring mediocrity of Princes Street, it is filled with fashionable boutiques, delicatessens and bistros. The Auld Hoose is the most traditional watering-hole along its length and I was sincerely hoping to find it as distinctive as the street itself.

The Auld Hoose is an old house but the manageress was uncertain as to how old it was. Asked about possible clues to its age she mentioned a tree that was inside the pub, but at the surprise expressed, admitted it was only a plastic tree. The pub looks old, a honeycomb of rooms set on two levels, lending a charm and privacy missing in many pubs. Partly because of this troglodyte effect and partly because of the decor, it is a dark pub. The rooms are decorated in traditional Victoria style—heavy velvet curtains, red leather chairs, orange gas lamps, dark grey walls interrupted by gilt-framed prints and copious amounts of brass.

The manageress prides herself on the mixed clientele—students, businessmen, the older generation, the hordes of rugby barbarians that come with the internationals. Perhaps it is because of the mixed clientele that this pub is not so strong on character as might be hoped. This said, it is a cosy pub where it is easy to sink down and idle away an evening, especially in winter when the sombre colours draw tight around you and thoughts of moving disappear down your glass. The beers are not particularly impressive, coming from the Alloa Breweries, and the only real ale they have is Arrol's.

THE HAYMARKET BAR

Standing opposite Haymarket Station, this large old pub is a confusing warren of separate booths and rooms radiating out from the oval bar in the centre. Stained glass, dark wood and mirrors proliferate and the newcomer should be wary of bumping into, and subsequently apologising to, their own reflection. The video and CD juke box may or may not be your idea of the ultimate in pub entertainment. If not, fear not. There are generally good jazz bands on Sunday nights.

The Edinburgh Association of Spiritualists have their headquarters just around the corner, though nobody could tell me if they were regulars or not. A middle aged man claimed to be one of their number and laughed. Perhaps he was just a happy medium.

In deference to the crowds who come to hear the jazz at the weekends, the Manager operates an over-25 rule on Friday and Saturday nights to keep out the young drinkers who are strangely attracted here.

PLATFORM ONE
The Caledonian Hotel
1 Princes Street

If you are in the mood for some McEwan's or a malt and a busy spot to while away the hours, then perhaps Platform One is the place for you. The crowd that packs the joint at the weekend were primarily in their 20s and 30s with a sizeable smattering of peroxide blondes.

Stephen Ewing, the Supreme Commander of the pub, is very friendly, as are the other servers. Although the decor was unamazing, Platform One does offer live rock on Saturdays as well as folk on Wednesdays and Fridays. Unfortunately, there isn't a dance floor here, so if you feel your feet tapping to the beat, walk on out and make for a club.

During the Festival, this establishment hosts the McEwan's Jazz performances and is open on Sundays as well.

RYRIE'S BAR
Haymarket Terrace

With its ornate wood and stained glass exterior and solid wood panelled interior, the basic lack of any pretension makes Ryrie's a shining example of a traditional Scottish pub. Dust and linoleum may long since have replaced spit and sawdust, but the old ambience, like many of the old customers, lingers on.

The pub has no unnecessary frills to it, no pseudo-Tudor beams or nostalgic artefacts. Instead, it has a long well-stocked bar, of great antiquity (150 years) serving a fine pint of McEwans 80/-. On Thursdays and Sundays, a variety of bands play in the upstairs lounge, ranging from folk to blues to country.

As the bar is situated at the fork where the road to Tynecastle leaves the road to Murrayfield, it is a popular Saturday stopover for those wanting to lay down the foundations of a good match atmosphere.

WEST END HOTEL
35 Palmerston Place

The West End, besides the area behind Charlotte Square, is not good for pubs. The majority of bars are to be found in hotels: characterless, quiet, undistinctive drinking places that all except residents avoid. However, I needed a drink and, given the hour, I was prepared to accept anywhere. In the end I made for my nearest bar, the West End Hotel.

As I gingerly made my way in, I became unsure whether the place was still operational. The barmaid informed us there was still half an hour left. In the corner was a small band strumming out traditional celtic folk tunes. The clientele was distinctive and when I asked the barmaid her opinion of the punters, she was determined in her reply, 'Highland'.

The whole bar exudes a Scottishness absent from other Edinburgh pubs—shinty sticks on the wall, a massive MacLean tartan drape partitioning off one part of the room, and on the wall, prints of crofters cutting the peat and planting potatoes and distillers involved in their time-honoured practice. The beers here do not amount to much. As this is a Highland bar, it is best you order whisky. You will have fun choosing.

There is live music here in Wednesdays, Fridays, Saturdays and Sunday—folk and Scottish country, needless to say.

The pub is close-knit and incredibly friendly, you can be sure of a converation here if you want one. The bar is open until 1am on Fridays and Saturdays.

INTRODUCTION TO THE SOUTHSIDE

To the south side of the Old Town is a stretch of land bordered on one side by Holyrood Park and on the other by Morningside Road. This area is as attractive as it is various. Morningside is the quintessentially middle-class district of Edinburgh. It is characterised by old ladies with blue rinses and the quietly civilized manners of all who live there. Down the road is the slightly more raucous district of Bruntsfield where the boutiques give way to curry houses and video shops. The flats are smaller and the cars are dirtier, but people have a good time.

To the east is Marchmont, where the tall, foreboding tenements are mainly occupied by students and young couples. The lack of good pubs in this area is an indication of the way these people party in the privacy of their home. Further down the Meadows the 'Greek-temple' houses in Sciennes are the final bastion of good taste and classical architecture before you get to the noisy and dirty Newington Road.

The Southside itself is a divided community. The boarded up shops and derelict buildings are an indication of economic hardship and a decayed and declining social shell. This was an area where printers and brewers did good business. However, the development of housing along The Pleasance and St Leonard's Street shows that the community is beginning to revive itself.

The result of this variety is that in some pubs you might find hordes of leather-clad professionals with their mobile phones sitting on the bar, in another you might find pensioners sitting around sipping dark ales and playing dominoes, and in another the hostile stares that greet you may mean that you never get past the door.

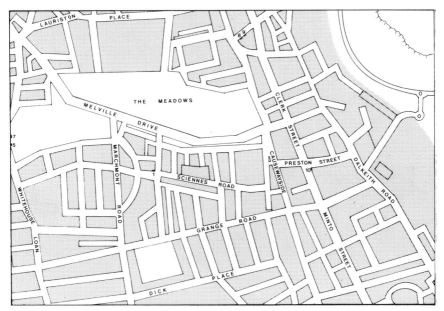

SOUTH EDINBURGH

1. The Argyle
2. The Auld Toll
3. Bennet and Son
4. The Cannyman
5. Chaplin's
6. The Links Hotel
7. Ye Olde Golf Tavern
8. The Peartree
9. The Partridge
10. The Wineglass

THE ARGYLE BAR
15 Argyle Place

Situated on the edge of the Meadows in suburban Marchmont, The Argyle has survived a recent refurbishment to remain a small and cosy bar with a traditional oak bar and furniture.

As The Argyle is owned by Belhaven Breweries, it sells Belhaven 70/- and 80/- (reasonably priced at 98p per pint), and the slightly unusual Belhaven lager. The pub's own specially brewed lager, imaginatively called 'Argyle Lager', is also well worth sampling, particularly in a 2 litre take-away cask! Quite unusually for Edinburgh, The Argyle does a reasonable pint of Guinness, but it is slightly over-priced at £1.20 per pint.

There is a good selection of non-alcoholic beers—Weizenthaber, LA Cider, L.A. Lager, Smithuichs Bitter—available, and the range of imported beers includes one fine Italian Birra Peroni. Freshly brewed coffee and good quality, though basic bar food, (mince and steak pies, toasted sandwiches, filled rolls etc.), are available throughout the day, with one unusual addition of jars of fresh mussels which are perfect for building up a thirst!

THE AULD TOLL
37-39 Leven Street
Bruntsfield

There has been a tavern sited here since the early eighteenth century—the name of the pub stems from the toll gates which used to stand on the highway outside until 1852.

The pub was completely refurbished last year though some of the older woodwork and general layout of the interior has been retained. The pub has a capacity of around 150 people, a popular feature being the alcove-type seating in the lounge—ideal for chatting or a little extra privacy.

The beers on tap are McEwan's 80/- and 70/- and Tartan. There is also Guinness plus various lagers including Beck's at £1.29 a pint and Harp.

The clientele is mixed but it is an 'older' rather than a 'young' pub. The regulars value the Auld Toll as an ideal place for a quiet chat in an atmosphere free from music. There is a one-arm bandit and a TV, used primarily to watch sport. The toilets are new, clean and pleasant with facilities for the disabled. The Auld Toll is located near the Kings Theatre and so car parking facilities are limited.

BENNET AND SONS
1 Maxwell Street

Down and out in blue-rinsed Morningside? Oppressed by the omnipresent powder-puffs and patent leather? Then head for Bennet's Bar, loosen your tie and your whale-boned corset, and relax in an atmosphere released from the airs and graces of the south-western sophisticates. Off the trendy-beaten black track, leaving the post-modernism to the Next man, and ignorant of the intellectual outpourings to be found around the Uni, this pub is a haven of blue vinyl, formica and bottle-end window panes.

You will have to look for this pub because, tucked away into the corner of Maxwell Street and Morningside Road, it is unimposing and unpretentious. Inside there is little charm, not a lot of comfort, the walls are smoke-stained and the toilets smell, yet a better indication of its warm cheeriness is given by the smiles, laughter and chatter of the customers.

The range of beers is adequate with Belhaven 60/-, 70/- and 80/- on draught as well as Murphy's stout, (114p for a pint), and Carlsberg lager (96p for a pint). White wine is most definitely not on offer. And cocktails? Come off it!

Except for the inevitable one-arm bandit, non-alcoholic distractions are sparse.

What you will find in Bennet's is the warmth and camaraderie of ordinary Edinburgh people who come here to drink a good, ordinary pint and discuss the events of their lives.

THE VOLUNTEER ARMS
(known as THE CANNY MAN'S)
237 Morningside Road

The Canny Man's is the nickname of the Volunteer Arms, an old establishment under the same management since 1879, which takes great pride in its long history. Much of this is on public display, the walls obscured from skirting board to ceiling with a vast eclectic collection of memorabilia, antiques, junk comprising over one hundred clocks, various stuffed animals, skis, and an Edwardian perambulator suspended precariously above the lounge.

It is claimed that each item is linked to the history of the pub and certainly much of this is connected with the officers of the corps of Volunteers, who frequented the Inn around the turn of the century. Apparently, during the winter months,

they would ski down the Old Biggar Road (now Morningside Road) from Fairmilehead right to the door. Local celebrities were also to be found here: the artist Joucser O'Daly papered the Old No 4 Room with copies of the London Illustrated News (dated 1874), and Sam Bough painted the inn sign which hangs in the main bar, to pay off his drinking debts.

Less attracted by the intrinsic interest, the more hygiene-conscious will probably pull out dusters and make a start right away, for not only are the walls covered with one hundred years of history, but the objects themselves are coated with a hundred years of dust. This has been described as a health hazard, a fire hazard, or merely a frustration for those whose fingers twitch at the thought of a quick once-over with the Mr Sheen. But beware, these objects are jealously guarded and anyone found souvenir hunting will be ejected. Be advised also that cameras are not allowed in the bar.

Other aspects of the pub which the management are at pains to promote—whether out of nostalgia or as a public relations exercise—are a cat named Sooky, their freedom from brewery tenure, and numerous traditions such as the coating of the floor with sawdust, the method of serving spirits by the ¼ gill, the house rule on serving gin and tonic (¼ gill gin, ice, lemon and Schweppes tonic), and the use of Pony glasses to serve water.

Families are provided with a games room, a garden room and a beer garden. Children's drinks are available at reduced cost. A car park is situated to the rear.

In the evenings, the pub is busy, hot and smoky. From Mondays to Thursdays, live folk bands play in the lounge and on the Thursday I was there, many drinkers told me they had come along specifically to hear the music. The atmosphere is friendly and animated, and one of the attractions is the little rooms, nooks and crannies, where you can sit and chat without people brushing past or spilling drinks on your head. The clientele is varied: students, tourists, locals, young office workers and most were enjoying themselves. There were no rowdy drunks.

The drinks are of good quality and it does not take long to be served—there are 2 bars and legions of bar staff. The general concensus was that the drinks are over-priced, most beers costing over a pound, and, for example, a lemonade and lime 74p. There is a wide range of Scottish and continental beers and over 30 malt whiskies are held on the gantry.

Difficulties with the management aside, the greatest asset of the Canny Man's is its uniqueness and informality. You won't find another pub like it in Edinburgh (or Scotland for that matter).

CHAPLIN'S
1 Barclay Place
Brunstfield

By coincidence, I found myself in Chaplin's on the hundredth anniversary of the great man's birth. No-one else seemed too perturbed.

The exterior is garish, but it is all much friendlier when you get through the door. The staff are pleasant and there is some interesting ale on draught (Beamish, Warsteiner and Claustaler). Tennent's Lager, 70/- and 80/- would still seem to be the best sellers, however.

The Chaplin theme does not run much further than a few posters, but the regulars do not seem too put out. The decor is functional (awaiting a 70s revival perhaps), and the carpet is definitely tartan. Deacon Blue would appear to be the sound of the moment. It does not seem to attract too much passing trade—but the regulars are welcomed personally and have certainly made this pub their own.

LINKS HOTEL
Bruntsfield

A red neon light announced the Links lounge bar through the Edinburgh night. This fact alone distinguishes it from street upon street of student flats on this side of town. Inside, it is all very far from the Young Ones.

Chart hits of the recent past are piped quietly in the front room. This has been recently refurbished in pink and red, with just a touch of chrome. It has a pleasant aspect, looking out over to Bruntsfield, and in summer you can sup your pints outside.

On the tap, there are some interesting additions to the usual McEwan's and Younger's, (Murphy's, Harp and Carlsberg are all available). Prices are reasonable and the bar is open until midnight all week. The Links is good for a quiet heart to heart, (actually, it's often so quiet that someone might hear you), as all of the younger, livelier regulars are to be found through the back.

There is a dark, smoky (atmospheric?) pool room, which seemed to be the main attraction for the regulars, who are all on good terms with the bar staff. The passing trade seems to confine itself to the front room.

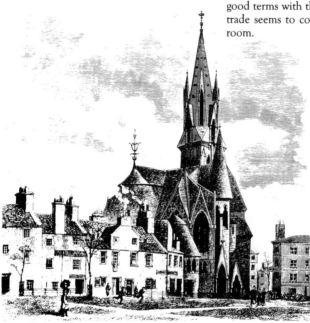

YE OLDE GOLFE TAVERN
31 Wrights Houses Bruntsfield

Set at the edge of the Bruntsfield Links, next to the Meadows, the Golf Tavern enjoys an extremely pleasant outlook. Legend relates that there has been a tavern here, facing the ancient golf course of Bruntsfield Links since 1399. In fact James Brownhill built the inn here in 1717, and this became the first tavern and later the clubhouse of the Royal Burgess Golfing Society.

It used to be a pub of great character where murderous golfers would congregate after some energetic pitch-and-putting on the Meadows. Nowadays there is a bit too much money knocking around. Young men come here to drink excessively, spill their drinks over everybody else, and re-enact Monty Python sketches. Beers on tap include the McEwan's range, Theakstons' Best Bitter and Old Peculiar, Greenmantle Ale, Becks, Harp and McEwan's lager, and a full selection of bottled beers.

The prices are slightly over the odds. The food selection is, however, impressive and the menu is similar to that of a good bistro. A continental breakfast is also offered.

The pub remains popular and can become very crowded, particularly on Thursday, Friday and Saturday nights. Whilst overhead fans dispel much of the smoke, it remains humid and quite noisy— not the ideal place for a quiet sit down and a chat.

THE PEAR TREE
38 West Nicholson Street

In 1749, this building was owned by William Usher, the same man who made his millions in brewing and left the city the large, but acoustically useless, Usher Hall across the meadows from the pub. After lying derelict for some time the building was rebuilt into a pub ten years ago.

The interior is dominated by a large island bar around which are scattered old tables and chairs that have been lifted out of various churches and gothic houses around the country. Lounging around on these chairs the freakier sections of society tend to waste the daylight hours and during the night the place is crammed with societies, clubs, fraternities, chums, and teams who all carve themselves a niche in the crowd which they protect with violence.

In one corner of the bar there is a coal fire and in another there is a food bar where unremarkable lunches are served between 12.00 and 2.00. In front of the pub there is a large courtyard with a scattering of picnic benches. More than a thousand people can be crammed into this space and during the summer months there are often that number until 2am when the licence ends.

THE PARTRIDGE
32 West Nicholson Street

The Partridge is next to the Pear Tree. No surprises there. Nor is there anything very remarkable about the decor of the place: mirrors, wood-panelling, green carpet, juke box, games machine, darts, drunken students avoiding classes, etc.

The Partridge does, however, claim to serve the cheapest drinks on the Southside and for that reason there is always a steady stream of determined drinkers flowing through the doors from 9.30am when it opens. It is a quiet place with no windows and is, therefore, a good place to retreat from the noisy and raucous pub next door. The standard of beer is also good and they serve a fine pint of Theakstons' Old Peculiar.

THE WINE GLASS
1-5 Newington Road

The Wine Glass is basically an unassuming local. The interior is nicely set out, filled with plenty of wood and shining metal to create a feeling of welcoming warmth which absorbs those who wander inside. The walls are filled with a variety of prints which engage the eye without seeming cheap, and the whole place is unpretentious and cosy.

There is no music to interfere with the flow of conversation of the local regulars and students, instead a cheerful hubbub of chat infuses the bar with life. The food is reasonably priced, although there are no special reductions, and there is a fairly wide stock of spirits, although no unusual beers.

The Wine Glass is open from midday to midnight, and whilst it is hardly the sort of pub to go out of the way to see, neither is it one to avoid.

FIGHTIN' DRUNK

INTRODUCTION TO LEITH

A Scottish historian noted in 1818 that 'from the rapid increase of intermediate buildings between Edinburgh and Leith, they will soon be identified as one city'. In the late 20th century most people forget the two were ever separate. An evening spent in Leith's taverns, however, reveals a community with a distinctive identity shaped by its own turbulent history.

The port's thriving trade and strategic position often made it a target of military attack. In 1559, Leith was besieged by the French after their Queen Regent made it her base. The English, too, assaulted Leith regularly—in 1313, 1410 and 1522. Henry VIII and 10,000 of his troops added to the list of aggressors by burning and pillaging the town in the 1540s.

Nor did Leith enjoy good relations with Edinburgh, which envied the port's prosperous soap, glass and cloth trades. A royal charter granting the port to Edinburgh in 1329 marked the beginning of Leith's long struggle to free itself from the authority of the capital city.

Leith, however, still remained Scotland's premier port. Merchant ships sailed regularly to industrial centres like Hull, Newcastle, Liverpool and Dublin, with the passage to London taking less than a week by 1820. It was so successful in the early 18th century that an English lord remarked that Leith, not Edinburgh, should be Scotland's capital city.

In 1790, Constitution Street was built to provide easier access to the busy docks. Leith Walk—originally a footpath—soon linked Edinburgh's newly-built North Bridge to Leith along the line marking Scotland's fortified stance against Oliver Cromwell and his army.

Leith may today be a sad reflection of its industrial past, but the spirit which built it lives on in its pubs. It was said to host four types of people a few centuries ago—mariners, maltmen, trades and traffickers. Add to that today, Jaguar owners, accountants, students and property developers. You may spend 30p rather than 3/6d to reach it from Edinburgh's city centre, but it takes only 15 minutes now—with no risk of meeting Cromwell on the way.

The Shore is still in many ways the focus of Leith pub life. Its shipping offices, warehouses and dockside inns have been replaced by dockland developments and smart new bars which provide the perfect start for any exploration of the area. The Shore was where the old Leith was born, and it is where the new Leith has begun.

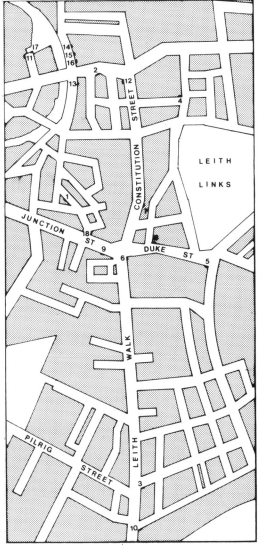

LEITH

1. The Bay Horse
2. Bernard's
3. The Boundary Bar
4. Bowler's Rest Bar
5. Carldon Lounge
6. Volunteer Arms
7. Checkers
8. The Duke's Head
9. Macpherson's
10. The Old Salt Inn
11. The Original Dock Tavern
12. The Port O' Leith
13. King's Wark
14. Pier's Point
15. The Shore Bar
16. The Trading Post
17. The Waterfront Wine Bar
18. Whitson's and Brown's

THE ARMS OF LEITH.

THE BAY HORSE
63 Henderson Street

The Bay Horse has been a landmark in Leith for over a hundred years, and its strikingly preserved Edwardian facade is still attracting visitors. The front retains its original stained glass windows, and the antique theme is continued by the framed series of old black-and-white photographs which capture the town as it was.

It's a pub which welcomes tourists and regulars alike. The prices are reasonable, and the hours long. It opens, in fact, from 9am, a characteristic less unusual in Leith than elsewhere.

All is not quite as it seems, however, and the pub's history is rather gruesome in parts. A previous owner hanged himself, the story goes, on realising the day was Bloody Sunday and that there was no-one in the pub. So you can't be sure if it's really a ghost that you see on a dark and windy night in Leith, or whether you've just imbibed more than you should have. It's worth a look at least, for those too timid to tarry.

BERNARD'S
Bernard Street

The street which gives Bernard's its name was built in 1777 to house the port's administration. In the 18th century it was the commercial centre of Franco-Scottish trade during the Auld Alliance, a time when there were Russian, Prussian and Danish Consulates in the area.

Bernard's itself was once a shipping company's accounts office. Its conversion to a drinking place set in motion something of an identity crisis. Opened originally as The Capercaille, the building used up a number of pub names and themes— including the headbashing 'Bonkers'— until its rebirth as Bernard's, a large, comfortable and very friendly bar/restaurant.

The look—and the food and drink prices—may be upmarket Edinburgh, but the welcome is unmistakably downtown Leith. The newly-wed owners, Gary and Maggi Butters, have created a honeymoon atmosphere as suited to jeans and sweat-shirts as it is to top-hat and tails.

Try to catch 'Maggi Sings Jazz' on

Wednesdays and Fridays, when she croons along to some delicate piano accompaniment. Bernard's Sunday Jazz brunches also offer alternative Sabbath entertainment. But any night of the week, Bernard's plush seats and easy-going atmosphere offer a quiet retreat from the more boisterous taverns nearby.

THE BOUNDARY BAR
379 Leith Walk

Leith this most certainly is—or Edinburgh, depending on what part of the pub you're in. For the Boundary Bar is exactly that: the frontier between Edinburgh and Leith runs across the middle of the floor.

In the old days the pub was divided into two. The Edinburgh half closed at 9.30pm, whilst Leith stayed open until 10pm. The busier Edinburgh side would spill into Leith for an extra half hour's drinking.

The original boundary plaque, previously built into the bar, now perches above the counter, still marking the border. Some of the regulars, most of whom have been coming here for at least ten years, still solemnly walk across the boundary to buy their last drinks.

Although everybody knows each other here, the Boundary has a very friendly atmosphere and tasty beer. There is the usual brigade of diehard Heavy drinkers but the pub also has its more sober characters. The pool table is the main centre of attraction.

The pub reputedly opens at 7am which might be a bit early for some, but not for Kenny who gives new meaning to the word 'regular'. He proudly showed me the old Leith entrance which has remained padlocked for many years. All the customers now use the Edinburgh door.

Everyone appears to stand everyone else drinks in some huge, confusing rota, so you find yourself buying pints for people you don't particularly like, and receiving them from people you've never seen before. Customers regularly serve themselves behind the bar.

Rivalry among pubs in Leith is keen. When I asked Kenny's opinion of The Old Salt, he was characteristically dismissive: 'Och ye dinnae want to go there, man. It's a hole in the wall'.

BOWLER'S REST BAR
Mitchell Street

At the end of Mitchell Street, one of Leith's most derelict and window-smashed alleys, is the small, white, McEwan's light of the Bowler's Rest Bar. It's like finding a lighted match in a pile of rubble.

Bowlers is a bar out of time: three wooden tables, two wooden chairs, and a long wooden bench face the bar. The walls are bare, the floor linoed. Behind the bar are four spirits and four draught beers at yesterday's prices: 68p for Bells, 92p for McEwan's Export and 98p for a locally-reknowned pint of Guinness. A plate of pie and beans costs 30p.

All that seems to have been added, in fact, since Lawrie Riley bought it thirty three years ago, is a TV, a fruit machine, an excellent pool table and a pin-up calendar on either side of the bar. Riley, among the youngest of the people there, was a member of Scottish football's 'Famous Five' in the late 1940s.

With the growth of business in the area, however, change may come. Riley has plans for a lounge, renovations, and snacks. Good news for Riley, perhaps, but it may take away some of the honest charm of what is reckoned to be one of Leith's oldest bars.

CARLDON LOUNGE, DUKE OF WELLINGTON
142 Duke Street

The Carldon Lounge is at the south end of the historic Leith Links, where Charles I once played golf. The locals say that the Links were the birthplace of the game, a claim which St Andrews, among others, would dispute.

The history of the Carldon Lounge is more sinister—many believe it is one of Leith's haunted pubs.

The building stands on the site of an old undertaker's and the last proprietor is said to have hanged himself in the cellar. It is his restless spirit that regulars fear haunts the place. A memorial stone erected above the gantry in his memory is now painted over but its outline remains faintly visible.

The ghost in the Carldon's cellar is taken very seriously by the locals, some of whom became upset and angry when the subject is raised. Those who would talk about it say that kegs and barrels have been known to move mysteriously across the cellar floor, while several claim to have witnessed the apparition.

The high turnover of management is also darkly attributed to the evil influence in the cellar. Regulars say that most Carldon landlords only stick the job for a while—then they 'freak out'.

Go there if you dare.

THE CENTRAL/
THE VOLUNTEER ARMS
7 Leith Walk

Described by one regular as 'one of the remaining focal points for old Leithers', the Central is a slice of local life.

The pub was built originally as Leith Central Station, and its interior retains many original features. The wall lamps and decorative tiles nostalgically recall a time when railway stations were more gracefully constructed.

The pub is commonly divided into two parts, left and right of the gantry, with the pool table at the back in what was once the waiting room. The right section is known as the 'good' side reserved for lively Leith chat and local gossip.

The left or 'rough' side provides the arena for 'Leith Rules' arm-wrestling. Two candles burning either side of the contestants' arms add that extra spice to the game. Losers stand to hurt more than their pride.

Telly addicts may recognise The Central from a recent series of Lager advertisements which were filmed in the bar because of its exceptionally high ceilings. Regulars boast that the bar has 'the highest ceiling in the East of Scotland'.

True to the spirit of Leith taverns, The Central's opening hours are generous— 7am-11pm on weekdays, with a late licence until 2am at the weekend. Friday nights feature two Go-Go dancers while dominoes are always available for those with a little less 'go'. OAPs can take advantage of special prices. A nip and a half will cost them only £1.

If you like your drinks cheaper than this, try The Volunteer Arms five minutes walk away. Known locally as the 'Volley'— referring to the time it was staffed by volunteers during the Great War—the bar's prices are unbeatable. Mixers are free, spirits are only 53p and all of the standard beers cost less than 90p.

CHECKERS
Constitution Street

Spectacular stained glass windows make the entrance to Checkers distinctive. The fact that those windows portray boats rather than biblical scenes reassured me that drinking here would have less of a damning effect on the mortal soul than smuggling a bottle of gin into Westminster Abbey.

Leith's proud heritage is displayed in the paintings of three-masted ships and the wooden models of 19th century clippers which perch above the bar. Checkers is a large pub made larger by the enormous mirrors hung between the sailing ships. If you go to a pub to see and to be seen, then this is the one for you.

All Checkers lacks is a large clientele. Although licensed until 1am it usually closes at midnight because of the lack of custom. This is a pity as Edinburgh could do with more bars as stylish as this.

THE DUKE'S HEAD
21 Duke Street and
THE MARKSMAN
13b Duke Street

The Duke's Head is the soul of Leith and a living shrine to Jimmy Miller. The cartoon above the spirit bottles proclaims the news that the former Rangers centre is now putting them over the bar as landlord. At 90p a pint and £1.20 a double, it is hard not to make a reflexive lunge.

This is a working man's bar. The icons on the wall hark back to Ibrox in the 50s and 60s, and the furnishings to Sparta several centuries B.C. (even before Jimmy Miller). The old men of Leith are the regulars. Their faces and their curses are as well worn as everything else in this bar, except the women's toilets. All strange men are foreigners. Any woman is an extra-terrestrial and if she ventures in here, even with a male companion, she is likely to experience an unsolicited close encounter.

A pilgrimage to the Duke's Head is obligatory for Rangers' fans and students of living religion—although supporters of Celtic and Hibs, who play at nearby Easter Road, worship here apparently without trouble.

Open everyday except the Sabbath, from 11 to 11, Jimmy gets in at 7pm on weeknights and 8pm on a Saturday. Mrs Miller does her best to prepare the way until then. God is fiftyish, short, and wears half a rollie behind his right ear.

Similar in clientele and furnishings in The Marksman, a few doors down. It is like a Spanish bar with bullfighting posters but without the Tapas.

MACPHERSON'S
5 Great Junction Street

MacPherson's is the first bar you see as you turn off Leith Walk onto Great Junction Street, which follows the line of the 1560 fortifications. Like many pubs in the area, it keeps ungodly hours. The doors open at 9am. Still, for anyone coming off a nightshift or simply wanting to get ahead of the day's drinking, a pint of Arroll's 80/- might make a welcome breakfast.

The bar's recent modernisation has attracted a relaxed mix of business types, younger trendies and solitary drinkers. Small table lamps in each booth add to the cosy atmosphere.

The traditional pub feel is maintained by lots of old wooden panelling, three feet of which fortunately protected me from the vicious looking Rottweiler dog which stands guard behind the bar.

Toasties are served throughout the day and the lunchtime menu is of the scampi and chips variety and starts at a reasonable £2.00. They stock a range of Alloa beers and Castlemaine lager on draft, Light at about £1, as well as a good selection of Scottish Malts and American bourbons by the ¼ gill.

MacPherson's probably does not merit a special trip, but is a handy local if you live in the area and a worthy port of call on any Leith pub crawl.

THE OLD SALT
17 Albert Place

As I entered the Old Salt, all heads swivelled in unison to examine the stranger. It was as though I was the first newcomer in fifty years. Perhaps I was.

Several things were immediately apparent. Apart from the barman and the sole woman present, I was the youngest there by a couple of decades. The Old Salt indeed—most of the characters looked like wizened old seamen.

Old pictures adorned the walls, giving a suitably venerable impression. But like a lot of working men's pubs in Leith, the television is always on. As I ordered a (very cheap) pint of beer, EastEnders blared out from the box.

The old-timers, their consumption of ale matched only by their energetic dart-playing, were clustered in the corner closest to the sole female drinker. There did not at first appear to be a women's toilet—then I spotted it away in the distance, a table blocking the entrance.

People who drink in these pubs seem to come from Leith first and Edinburgh second. The old man I was speaking to said he had not been 'north of the border' (between Edinburgh and Leith) for a couple of years. His huge beer gut certainly indicated how long it was since he had last been out of The Old Salt. The pub still opens at 6am according to the locals.

Eastenders finished and Last of the Summer Wine began. As I left I realised that I had been the only person who'd had to ask for a drink. Everyone else had just looked at the barman.

THE ORIGINAL DOCK TAVERN
314 Dock Place

The Dock Tavern is a genuine 'local', a rare find in Leith's fashionable area. More relaxed and less self-consciously trendy than some other dockside watering holes, it boasts a warm atmosphere and a regular clientele, including a cat called Oliver.

Although it offers some high quality and reasonably priced food, the emphasis is firmly upon being a pub rather than a Bistro. The McEwans 80/- is well taken care of and there is a wide array of imported beers, wines and whiskies. Look out for the rum—there is a selection of nine brands featuring several lethal 100 proof bottles.

The pub's history is colourful. Ten years ago its position opposite the dock gates still assured it a steady stream of thirsty dockers. Its fortunes, however, declined with those of the docks, and the brewery closed it down in 1986.

It was bought in 1988 by Peter and Avril Smith, two native-born Leithers, who have taken it upmarket without losing touch with the pub's past. Decorated in a nautical theme, it retains original gaslight fittings and an old pressure gauge behind the bar from the days when the beer was pumped up from the cellar using water power.

The dockers may have all long disappeared, but the Original Dock Tavern is here to stay.

PORT O' LEITH
58 Constitution Street

This Leith is a world away from the smart and costly Shore area. Locals and sailors lounge beneath naval flags tacked to the roof which recall Leith's proud history as Scotland's busiest port.

No Jaguar-driving yuppies here—the tables are covered with humble green plastic and a 'Don't Pay the Poll Tax' sticker takes pride of place in the Ladies' loo. 'What's your name, hen?' crooned a woman rather the worse for wear, as I collected my half lager from the bar and escaped to the relative safety of a vinyl-clad seat.

An incongruous note was struck by the barman—who looked as if he would be more at home in London's Soho Brasserie—and by the reggae music issuing softly from behind the counter. The locals seemed to like both, however, and such inconsistencies only added to the pub's atmosphere. It deservedly won a profile two years ago in The Observer.

Food and drink is cheap here, and the visitor feels privileged in being seen as a novelty to be entertained. The Port o' Leith is a necessary antidote to an evening by the Shore.

Don't leave the area without dropping by the Quality Bar. Situated in the street of the same name, this clean and unfussy pub offers an extraordinary range of Scottish malts—almost 50 bottles stand proudly on top of the mirrored bar. Drinking lager in this tavern should be considered immoral.

Leith Waterfront

KING'S WARK
36 The Shore

The King's Wark has a history which perhaps merits more prominence in the recently renovated pub. Built on the site of the royal palace of Leith, it is said to have slept five kings and a queen in its time.

Its cellars have been used as an arsenal, and for the storage of wine and grain since the 15th century. Its fortunes declined, however, over the years, and prior to its destruction and rebuilding in the early 18th century it was used as a convalescent hospital for victims of the plague.

Until recently, the King's Wark was known in Leith lore as 'The Jungle', so called, in the words of a taxi-driver, because you could see the bodies flying out of the windows before you got there. The cellars were so dirty even the rats wore overalls, despite the terms of James VI's decree that a cellar be kept for the storage of the crown's provisions.

Times move on, however, and eighteen months ago the building's fortunes changed once more. A complete refurbishment drove its former inhabitants several yards up the road to the Drawbridge, where the only change made in recent years has been the re-upholstery of the uncomfortably narrow seats in beige-grey vinyl.

All that remains of the King's Wark's history are the rough-hewn walls and mysterious portrait, thought to be of the Young Pretender. The refurbishment has, however, been beautifully executed and the impression is of friendly, uncluttered warmth.

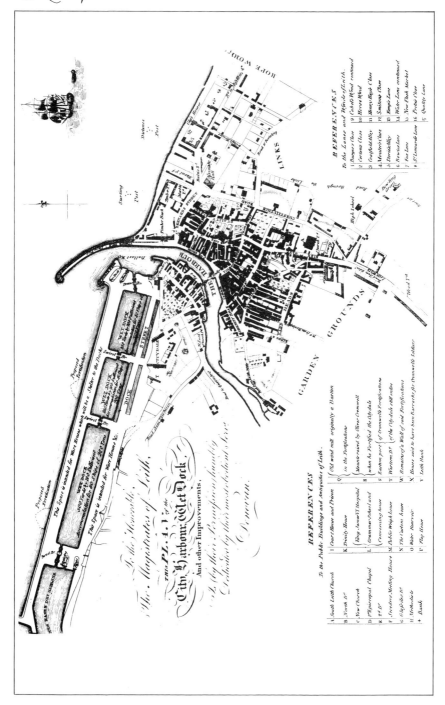

PIER'S POINT
1 The Shore

It's hard to imagine, as you sit in the bright modern surroundings of Pier's Point, that the building once played an important part in the long and varied history of the port.

Located at the northern extremity of The Shore, the pub was a signal tower during the Napoleonic Wars, guiding battleships and merchantmen safely into the harbour. This part of Piers Point's history is only evident in the gentle curve to the walls; not even a generous smattering of photographs of lighthouses can retrieve its active past.

All that remains to commemorate George IV's historic landing in front of the building in 1822—the first Scottish visit by a British monarch for 150 years—is a small plaque outside.

If most of Pier's Point maritime character has been taken out of it, what remains is an attractive, if not particularly special, watering hole. It has a good stock of foreign beers and serves above average pub grub at above average prices. In short, it is like any upmarket pub anywhere, and lacks the warm welcome of its Shoreside rivals.

THE SHORE BAR
3 The Shore

From the first glance at the front door—which says 'TUG' instead of 'PULL'—you know the Shore is a place of character. Its simple but cosy interior still bears resemblance to its days as a deep dark Leith pub, but the large mirrors give it a deceptive sense of space.

One of The Shore's best points is its live music. Jazz, blues and traditional folk is played every night of the week (except Sunday) at a volume that compliments the relaxed surroundings.

The Shore is a place for lively talk, a spirit confirmed by some fine Nationalist grafitti in the toilets ('1740s Demoralised, 1840s Balmoralised, 1992 De-Anglicised?')

The restaurant adjoining the bar serves some of the most reasonably priced (£12 per head) and delicious Scottish seafood in town, and its popularity means it is booked up 2-3 weeks in advance. The same food can however be sampled barside as well, served by an efficient and friendly staff. They also take some credit for feeding the flourishing swan population in the Water of Leith, just a few steps away—through, naturally, a door marked 'SHOVE', not 'PUSH'.

THE TRADING POST
32/34 The Shore

Never has a pub managed so successfully to dissociate itself from the history of its area. A small step through the door is a giant step away from Leith and into the Wild West. The bemused visitor is greeted by a lifesize Indian astride a horse which demands firewater for the chief and a drink for the little boy who swings from the hayloft.

'Mind Your Scalp' warns a sign above the bar from which is served frozen Margueritas, and the only draught Budweiser in town. The barmaids wear pink gingham skirts; the men Jack Daniels T-shirts and holsters. Dull red light catches the eyes of the stuffed racoon perched atop the roof of a shopfront behind the sidewalk-cum-stage.

The illusion of the great Western Outdoors is marred by the regulation fire extinguishers and exit signs. 'Have One for the Road': a scantily clad lady in Belle Hart's Whorehouse beckons to Brad, the lounging Mountie at the top of the stairs. A vast screen on the first floor plays John Wayne movies, and the ceiling is sky blue.

Before the Trading Post was taken over and refurbished to the tune of £300,000, it was the Highlife Disco, frequented by lowlife, as the legend goes. It is sad to think that it will soon be one of a hundred Trading Posts, if all goes to plan. Nonetheless, the Old Turkey, 'lunatic' country music and the dance floor nestling between the Indian and the Sidewalk, makes the place as wild, if not wilder than the West.

WATERFRONT WINE BAR
1c Dock Place

Bigger and more unashamedly trendy than the Old Dock Tavern opposite, the Waterfront's music is louder, as are some of its customers. There is, however, a fine selection of imported beers (including Brahmn lager from Brazil—get drunk and save the rain forest), and some rare malt whiskies. Here at last is a wine bar which takes its vocation seriously—there are more than 80 brands to choose from and special offers each month.

In the old days, the Waterfront was a waiting room for ferry passengers. The renovation 7 years ago has been sympathetic to its heritage, keeping the old stone work with wooden fixtures and Edwardian memorabilia. It offers enough secluded corners in which to escape stray Sloanes.

There is a heavy emphasis on food here. Only diners are admitted at lunch time, (12-2.30pm) at which time it teems with businessmen. Dogs, and children under five are excluded at all times (presumably in the name of hygiene). If you can, sit through the back which is usually reserved for diners. The views over the dock front are unusual for a pub. Drinkers can also sit outside and watch the port, a real treat on sunny days.

WHITSON AND BROWN'S
1 Henderson Street

Whitson and Brown's is a shrine to old Leith, fittingly situated close to where the old Kirkgate thoroughfare once provided the main route to the docks.

The old bakery ovens set into the wall are a reminder of the times when the building sold bread rather than beer to the local community. The counter—made from the upturned end of a boat—and the pictures of old Leith adorning every wall recall the town's more prosperous times as a bustling harbour.

Naturally, for a pub which seems more of a museum, the barman is the oldest exhibit of all. Now at the fine age of 88, Mr Whitson may also be the oldest publican in Leith.

INTRODUCTION TO OUTLYING DISTRICTS

For most visitors to Edinburgh, the city consists of the area between Holyrood Palace and the Castle with the Royal Mile in between and the New Town to the north. But this idea does not do justice to the different communities which are scattered about the area which Edinburgh now covers.

Over several centuries the city has spread and the boundaries between the city and its peripheral villages have melted away: Dean Village, Colinton, Newhaven, Greenside, Duddingston, Queensferry, Cramond and Leith are all examples of this effect. However, the individual character of these places does live on and often one can find tranquility and beauty in these historic districts.

Outside Edinburgh the countryside begins very quickly and it takes only a few minutes driving from the suburbs before one is in the green fields near Penicuik or along the beachy coasts near Aberlady. The quality of life in Edinburgh is greatly enhanced by those people who take the trouble to explore the hills, villages and sea-side around the capital. One can enjoy high-ridge walking more than a thousand feet up in the Pentlands and still be in sight of the city. Or else one can set sail in a dinghy or windsurfer from the beaches at Gullane and still be in sight of the factories at Portobello. These are privileges few city-dwellers can enjoy and go to make Edinburgh such a good place to live.

The Athletic Arms
Cramond Inn
Sheep's Heid Inn
Flotterston Inn
Habbie's Hawe
Hawe's Inn
Howgate
Leadburn
Liberton
Old Club House
Ship Inn

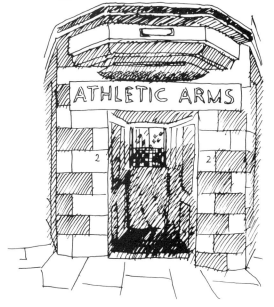

THE ATHLETIC ARMS (DIGGERS)
1 Angle Park Terrace

The Good Beer Guide describes this famous pub with just one word: Mecca. I cannot argue with that. Anyone who enjoys their beer has probably made a pilgrimage up the Gorgie Road to the Diggers, and once they have tasted the beer few people can resist going back.

The pub itself is housed in an unassuming building. It is a few moments from the Hearts home ground and so a few pictures of the most famous Hearts players are allowed up, but apart from that the place is a bit dank. The decorations inside are positively spartan. There are few diversions from the business of beer drinking except for some tables in the back for dominoes.

Mr Farmer, the bar manager, makes no apologies: 'The entertainments are the clients themselves. Conversation is the background music.' Everybody can remember the day Mr Farmer began his job here. It was in the second weekend of April 1962, the same day that Scotland beat England at Wembley.

But it isn't interior decorating or team loyalty that brings so many people here every night that they need a dozen bar staff to keep everyone happy. It is the McEwan's 80/- Traditional Ale, stored at a special temperature that only Mr Farmer knows and lovingly pulled through sparkling pipes that are cleaned every day, which makes this place so popular. The beer is silky smooth, with a creamy head and a fresh after-taste. It is indescribably good. The only thing I can suggest is that you get on a number 30 bus and ride up to Angle Park Terrace to taste for yourself. But be careful of your timing, the place shuts at 10.30.

CRAMOND INN
Cramond

Cramond village was originally built in 1780 for a mill workers' community who used the water-power from the River Almond to great advantage. Nestled in a hollow at the river's estuary the village retains a sense of isolation. All the buildings have whitewashed walls and black window frames, and I doubt if there have been any changes to the place since it was first built.

From the pub you can visit Roman ruins, which date back to Antonius Pius (AD 142) and the building of the Antonine Wall, bordering the village and stretch into the car park itself, or else you can walk up the River Almond which will eventually take you to the Union Canal and into Ratho. In the village, the Cramond Kirk is worth a visit, and so is Dalmeny House to the East. At the bottom of the village is a small dock where sailing enthusiasts can launch their dinghies.

The interior of the pub is disappointingly plain. The round tables and brown walls are far from inspiring but the atmposhere can more than make up for this. There is a positiviely hearty feel to the place on a windy afternoon when ruddy cheeks and tousled hair single out those who have been strolling by the sea. Waterproofs and rubber boots distinguish those who have been sailing.

At lunchtime, food is available from a separate bar against the back wall. The pub food available is uninspiring, but next door to the bar is a much more impressive restaurant which has especially good fish food. The beer is another compensation for the decor. Since the pub was recently sold to an English brewery there is a wide variety of beers from the South including, strangely, Newquay stout from Cornwall.

DUDDINGSTON LOCH & VILLAGE
FROM QUEENS' DRIVE.

THE SHEEP'S HEID INN
Duddingston

Tucked away beneath the plug of Arthur's Seat, this delightful village overlooks a beautiful loch which is home to a huge number of ducks, swans and other rare birds. The name of the village's inn comes from an embellished ram's head which is said to have been presented to the landlord of the pub by James VI of Scotland in 1590. One of James's descendants, Bonnie Prince Charlie is said to have slept before the battle of Prestonpans in a building nearby.

The inn itself is a splendid place to rest after you have walked around the parks and the village. There is a well stocked bar serving Tennent's beers and in the next room there is a lounge area where soups, salads, pies, steaks etc. are served at lunchtime.

To the rear there is a skittle alley which claims to be the oldest in Scotland. Not to be missed is the summer barbeque in the enclosed garden. As you sit amongst the bushes, around a teeming goldfish pond, the whiff of charcoal gently deuces your taste buds, and you will not be disappointed when your food arrives.

THE FLOTTERSTON INN
A(702) Towards Biggar

Steve Rzonca, a New York expatriate, recently re-opened the Flotterston Inn after a period of radical refurbishment. Though situated close to the main road (A720) it provides a welcome retreat for passing travellers and weary city-folk in the heart of the Pentland Hills.

The Inn is housed in a small, whitewashed Borders farmhouse half of which dates back to 1620 when, in the words of the landlord, 'it used to be a kinda lay-by station for the coaches to Biggar'. Since then Robert Louis Stevenson apparently based his walks in the Pentlands from the Inn and Rabbie Burns used to meet his Penicuik mistress here.

The bar itself is nice enough with a smart and clean decor, but the real attractions of this place are the hill walking and the garden. Around this area there are a number of great trails including those which lead to the Castlelaw Fort, House of Muir, Balerno and a popular trip to another good pub, Habbies Howe. The garden is well sheltered from the road and is a splendid place to enjoy yourself in the summer. There is enough room for children and other small animals to play around, and the small brook at the bottom gives the whole place a very peaceful ambience.

The clientele tends to be a mixture of regulars from Morningside and groups of enthusiastic hill walkers who come to enjoy a pint and a bite to eat after their hiking. In addition to the smart restaurant next door there is also an imaginative selection of pub food in the bar itself. The beers available are chilled in the American way, but you don't hear any complaints in the summer: Drybrough's 70/-, Alloa 70/-, foreign and bottled, etc.

HABBIES HOWE
Ninemileburn

If you're looking for a Laura Ashley-style farmhouse pub then try somewhere else. This is the genuine article, practically unchanged since Wullie, one of the regulars, used to deliver milk here fifty years ago. The nicotine-yellow walls are, however, decorated with dusty old bric-a-brac introduced to give the place some tone: a dead duck, some Bentley headlights, bridles, muskets, etc. Robby couldn't understand the need for it all, 'it's to gie the barmaid some dustin to do, I suppose'.

The small bar is as cosy as you'd want. There's a coal fire and a friendly barmaid to make you feel warm and welcome. The regulars are also cheerful. There are portraits of the eight staunchest drinkers at the pub hanging on the wall, and, for most of the time, the people themselves are sitting below, glass in hand.

On the wall above the bar is some writing. Wullie told me, 'they're lines from the "Good Shepherd" by Allan Ramsay. A wee laddie from Penicuik came in one night in 1948 and wrote them up there. I canna remember his name right now, but I will in a mo'.

The stables of this old coaching inn have been converted into a small restaurant serving great steaks, I was assured. The beers include Tennent's 80/-, Tennent's 70/-, Taunton Blackthorn, Guinness, L.A. and a variety of bottled beers. Take note of the Tennent's font, which must be as old as the bar.

The pub is thirteen miles south of Edinburgh on the A702 opposite the Nine Mile Burn petrol station. Apparently the local gibbet used to hang where the petrol station is now, which is worth thinking about when you are walking back to your car late at night.

HIC
QUAK

THE HAWES INN
South Queensferry

The Hawes Inn is a gleaming, white building standing on the edge of the Firth of Forth beside the small harbour at South Queensferry. Robert Louis Stevenson immortalized the place in his novel, *Kidnapped* which he wrote in 1886 while gazing out across the Forth from his bedroom (No. 13 in the Inn). Sir Walter Scott also mentions it in *The Antiquary*.

Davie Balfour would still find it a romantic place. The village itself has a secluded feel about it and overhead, the Forth Rail Bridge spans across the Inn so that one feels enclosed on all sides.

Inside the pub there are a number of rambling rooms where copious quantities of good food and drink are available throughout the day. There is an upmarket restaurant in the hotel as well as pub-food available in the bar. Beers include Burtons and Arrolls, Skol, Guinness, 70/-, Special, Export and Swan Light. There's a garden outside with a climbing frame as well as board games and darts in the bar.

During the week, the hearty regular crowd is peppered with young couples from the city attracted by the anonymity and romance of the place. During the weekend, the village is often filled with people sailing their boats, visiting the inn and seeking refuge from the city. Opposite the inn is the dock of the *Maid of the Forth* which travels to Inchcolm Abbey, a beautiful medieval monastery on an island in the middle of the Forth. On Friday nights in the summer the Maid sets sail with a jazz band. Tickets available by ringing 331 1454.

THE OLD HOWGATE INN
Nr Penicuik, Midlothian

The Howgate is an excellent inn which attracts an enthusiastic group of regulars during the week: rugby playing farmers, countrified solicitors, officers from the Redford Barracks, etc. At the weekend, hordes of grey-faced city dwellers fill the pub after roaming around the beautiful countryside.

Good food, first-class beer and a great deal of history are what makes this small country pub so popular. A record exists of pilgrims at an inn on this site as early as 1450. The present inn was built in 1743 to serve the coach which plied between Edinburgh and Dumfries. The mantle above the wood fire in the bar dates back to that time.

The service at the inn was not always as good as it is now. Sir Walter Scott referred to Jenny Dodds, who was landlady in his time, as a 'notorious slattern'. Things hadn't changed much by 1950 when the inn was sold for £300 and the new owner put down a stone floor for the first time.

Nowadays the bar is snug and friendly. It serves a wide variety of beers: McEwan's 80/-, Belhaven 80/-, Timothy Taylor Best Bitter, Theakstons' Old Peculiar, Taunton Cider and Carlsberg. There is a good variety of malts served in ¼ gills. You might also try the Danish Akvavit.

Next door to the bar is a very nice, though rather pricey, restaurant which specialises in farmhouse food and Smorgesbrod, Danish open sandwiches made with pickled fish. One of the regulars recommended the lobster which gives you an idea of the tone of the place.

THE LEADBURN INN
Leadburn, Peeblesshire

An inn has stood on this site since 1777 serving the travellers heading for Carlisle. John Buchan described it in *John Burnett of Barnes* as, 'the most villainous, bleak place that I have ever seen, and I who write this have seen many.'

He must have been referring to the public bar. That remains a pretty grim hole with a couple of disused pot-bellied stoves in the middle of the room to give it an 'earthy atmosphere', as the landlord describes it.

The rest of the pub is much more cheerful. In the last four years the successive owners have added a comfortable, slightly plush, public lounge and a concrete patio. Good food is available throughout the day in the bars and there are hotel rooms upstairs. The strange thing about the pub is a railway carriage tacked onto the side of the building which acts as the dining room for a smart, a la carte restaurant.

The beers served are Herriot 80/-, Tennent's 80/-, Tennent's Special, Tennent's Lager and Guinness. To get to the Leadburn, take the road going due south of Edinburgh (A701) through Penicuik until the junction with the Carlisle road and you'll find it there. Or else take the Eastern Scottish bus No. 62 with Melrose on the front.

THE LIBERTON INN
90 Kirkbrae

The Liberton was recently bought by Tennent who have changed it from being a spit and sawdust pub into a welcoming and comfortable place to enjoy a pint. The inn consists of three very different bars and a small, rather expensive restaurant.

The wood-pannelled public bar is a place where one can play dominoes, watch soccer and enjoy a drink with friends in the evening. The bar is decorated with the trophies won by the pub's various social clubs in a number of sports: fishing, golf, darts, bowling, etc. The atmosphere in the evenings is genial, in an alcoholic sort of way.

The middle bar is named the Rubens Butler Room after the indolent, but friendly, husband of Jeannie Deans in Sir Walter Scott's novel *The Heart of Mid-lothian*. Butler is supposed to have stayed in an inn on the site of the Liberton and one can suppose that Scott himself probably stayed a night here. The bar is decorated with stained glass, hunting pictures and stuffed birds which gives it a distinguished, if slightly morbid, feeling.

The third bar is by far the plushest of the lot. It has a thick red carpet, leather sofas and a collection of memorabilia hanging on the walls which includes books, china, hunting-horns and oil paintings. The building used to be a dairy, though you would not believe it now.

The beer served includes Pale Ale, Tennent's 80/-, Export, Special L.A. and Guinness.

THE OLD CLUB HOUSE
East Link Road, Gullane

Gullane is a small village on the banks of the Forth between Musselburgh and North Berwick. This part of the country is characterised by white beaches, rocky outcrops and innumerable golf links. The beaches at Gullane are very beautiful and many people come to swim, surf and walk when the weather is fine. The bird sanctuary at Aberlady and the palladian country house at Gosford are additional attractions.

The Old Club House has recently been refurbished to cater for the influx of trade from the city. It sits on the edge of Gullane Golf Course and overlooks the hills of East Lothian. It was originally built in 1890 as the golf course's club house, and it is decorated inside with all kinds of memorabilia from those days. As well as golf clubs, photographs, balls etc., the interior is decorated with artefacts from Victorian times proclaiming the supremacy of the British empire: placards advertising Rajah cigars and Cadbury's Cocoa, photographs of public schools, and so on. An old copy of *Tom Brown's School Days* finishes the impression of colonial grandeur and pomposity.

During the week, the bar tends to be full of golfers from the links, lounging around in the deep armchairs and talking about their missed putts and the problems of finding good caddies in these lean Thatcher years. At nights the wine bar and brasserie next to the lounge bar are very popular, and at weekends the whole place is full of families who have retreated from the rigours of the beach to the warmth of a wood fire.

THE SHIP INN
Ratho

Though the building was built around 1750, the Ship Inn only came into existance when the Union Canal from Edinburgh to Glasgow was constructed in 1822. Competition from trains killed the trade on the canal and it was officially closed in 1965. Since that time the Inn has changed from being a bar for the workers on the water to tank themselves up after a long day's work to being a family-oriented pub with a variety of distractions for people of all ages.

As well as two canalbarge restaurants, the Bridge Inn offers for hire boats of all sizes with or without bar, navigator or electric organ. Inside, the inn has been totally refurbished over the last year. The restaurant area has been extended and the bar has been moved to the back of the building. There is a thick carpet and comfortable chairs. The pub welcomes children and provides a room where they can join their parents to eat and there is a playground outside.

The Bridge Inn has a macabre connection. In 1846, George Bryce, who lived at the inn, killed a cook, Jane Seton, who had advised a friend not to consider marriage with Bryce as she felt him to be a dull fool. After a trial in the capital he became the last man to be publicly hanged in Edinburgh.

BREWERIES WITH TOURS AVAILABLE

Most breweries will allow tours on their premises. However, these trips normally need to be organized by the brewer's sales representative or through the landlord of a pub. Here are a list of contact numbers to help you organize trips:

SCOTTISH BREWERS

There is a free tour of the Fountain Brewery, organized by Maxine Mendelson. It leaves from the Gilmour Park entrance of the Brewery twice a day, at 10.30 and 2.30 Monday to Friday. The tour consists of a one hour guide around the place followed by refreshment and a video. Places for parties of no more than twenty people are bookable in advance on 229 9377.

THE ROSE STREET BREWERY

Tours of the fermentation process and other parts of this minute brewery are conducted by the eccentric Masterbrewer, Ron Brorscuzi, from Monday to Friday between 11.00 and 3.00. For further details and to book places in advance telephone 220 1227.

TENNENT'S

Tours can be organized through pubs and hotels by phoning Marie Sommerville on 334 3361.

BELHAVEN

Tours are arranged only for people in the trade or for those with an academic interest in brewing. Details may be obtained from Mrs Betty Porteous on (0368) 62734.

ALLOA

Trips are available only for people in the trade and are conducted through the sales division. Phone Mr Eaton on (0259) 723 539.

MUSIC

You would normally think of going to a concert hall to listen to music, and Edinburgh has a good selection of venues for these events. In the recently refurbished Usher Hall, you can listen to symphonies and concertos in grand surroundings. At the other end of town, The Playhouse, an inhospitable place, is a venue for bands and gigs for those with more contemporary tastes.

But it is in the pubs of Edinburgh where people can be seen to obviously enjoy their music. At a time when Scotland's own culture is on the defensive against attacks from the monolithic force of televised advertising and trans-Atlantic opinion-fixing, folk traditions have retreated to the institutions where the people, and not the images, are important.

All around Edinburgh, pubs play host to musicians. Some landlords organize special nights for bands and artists to play. Others encourage more spontaneous ensembles to perform as the mood takes them. It is at these events, where the enthusiasms of the performers combine with the participation of the crowds that the best fun is to be had. Often a few regulars will start the evening's performance, playing a few set pieces or practicing a new one together. But as the evenings wears on and the alcoholic consumption begins to have its effect, a few novices might try their hand learning techniques from the more experienced players and adding new songs to the repertoire. Before long, a band will have formed, shifting and changing in form as more people arrive and others take a break. At this point the participation of the spectators becomes important. A few might start to sing, the rest could dance and jig. The energy of this mass of people is enough to keep the musicians playing until late into the night.

It is at nights like these that the importance of the pub, as a place for people to get together to relax, and as a repository for folk arts such as music, becomes apparent. It is, therefore, rewarding to witness the number of pubs which give space to performers grow. It is also refreshing to visit the prestigious Edinburgh International Folk Festival which is held every year at the end of March. It is at this time that the general public can gain access to a culture which is rapidly disappearing. Because of the covert nature of these folk meetings we have put together a list of pubs which regularly hold musical evenings and Ceilidhs for those who want to join in.

FORREST HILL BAR

This is the second home of the Scottish Studies Department at Edinburgh University and as such plays a crucial role in the revival of interest in the Scots language in the post-War years. The most remarkable thing about this place is the way people fill the pub at any time of the day and it is not unusual to find a party going on at lunch time.

THE GREEN TREE

One of a pair of pubs in the Cowgate, the Green Tree has maintained a loyal following because of its landlord's determination to maintain high standards of beer, as well of music, during the lean years of the 60s and 70s.

BANNERMANS

The second musical pub in the Cowgate, and certainly the most extraordinarily decorated. The music here is not just folk, but also jazz and classical. I once sat next to a man playing a large piece of sheet metal hung from his shoulder during a particularly informal jamming session.

THE JUNCTION BAR

This place has particularly lively sessions on Friday nights, hosted by some of Edinburgh's 'weel-kent' folk musicians with help from visiting guests.

THE HEBRIDES

Being close to Waverley Station must make the players from the Highlands feel nearer home for they congregate here in large numbers. A popular place amongst Gaelic speakers, it is not unusual to see a set of pipes being passed around with each player being called upon to give a tune.

THE WEST END HOTEL

Nearer Edinburgh's other station at the Haymarket, the West End Hotel has organised music nights at the weekend, but during the week many Gaelic speakers congregate here and often pipes and fiddles are produced from under the tables as the evening goes on.

ENSIGN EWART

You are advised to get there early because this is not a big pub and when the music is playing, people are very reluctant to leave so the place gets very filled up.

OTHER PLACES

The Haymarket: jazz night on Sunday's
Ryries: anything from folk to blues. Thursday and Sunday
Candlemaker Arms: Scots and Irish folk, especially Thursday, Friday and Saturday
Negotiants: live bands
White Hart Inn: some music every night
Preservation Hall: mainly rock
Cannyman: every night

GAY BARS AROUND EDINBURGH

The Laughing Duck
24 Howe Street
225 6711

Key West
Jamaica Street

Chaps
Opposite the Playhouse on the Leith roundabout.

Millionaires Disco
Niddrie Street
558 1476
Open till 6.00 at weekends

Toppo's
1 Grindlay Street
Only on a Sunday

The Northumberland
1 Northumberland Street
556 2760

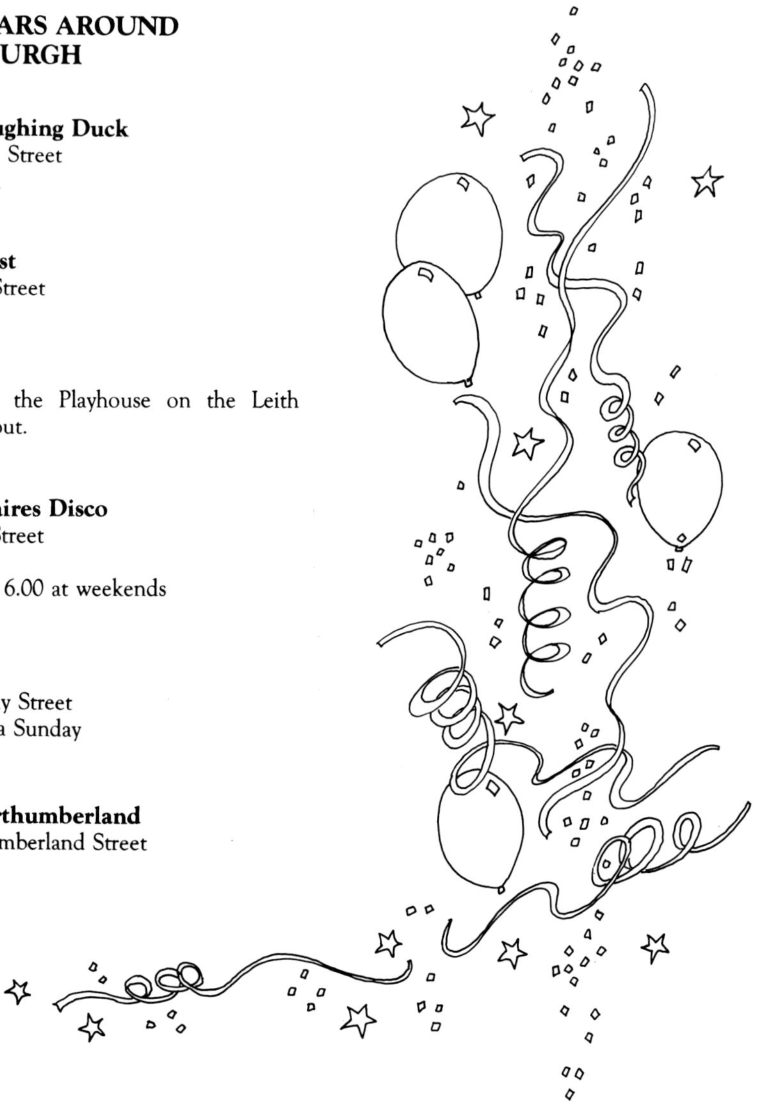

BIBLIOGRAPHY

Edinburgh David Daiches (Granada 1980)

People's Palaces—Victorian and Edwardian pubs in Scotland Rudolph Kenna & Antony Mooney (Paul Harris Publishing 1983)

Old Edinburgh Taverns Marie Stuart (1952)

The New Beer Guide Brian Glover CAMRA (1988)

Victorian Pubs Mark Girouard (1975)

GLOSSARY OF
SCOTS WORDS

aquavitae old name for whisky.
Athole brose honey and oatmeal mixed with whisky.
bead a glass or quantity of spirits: *He has a good bead in him.*
brak a bottle open a new bottle.
barley bree whisky.
dram a drink of liquor (especially) whisky, of any size.
drappie a drink.
export applied to a superior-quality beer, slightly darker in colour than **heavy.**
gantry a bottle stand in a bar.
hauf a half-measure of a specified amount, especially a half-gill of whisky, **a wee hauf** a quarter gill, a small whisky, **a hauf and a hauf** a small whisky with a half pint of beer as chaser.
heather ale a drink brewed from heather, hops, barm, syrup, ginger and water; the exact recipe was lost, so you are unlikely to find it in your local pub!
heavy *of beer* corresponding to English bitter, **wee heavy** a type of strong beer, usually sold in small bottled of ⅓ of a pint (approx 0.2 litre).
John Barleycorn ale or whisky.
light applied to a low-gravity beer (the successor of mild).
magnum (bonum) · a bottle containing two quarts (2.27 litres) of wine or spirits.
mountain dew old name for whisky, especially if illicitly distilled.
nappie *of ale* foaming strong; a strong ale.
pale ale, *formerly* **India Pale Ale** a kind of low-gravity beer.
plunk the sound of a cork being drawn from a bottle, a popping sound.
pundie a strong type of beer; liquor in general; a measure of beer given free to brewery workers.
quaich a shallow bowl-shaped drinking cup, originally made of wooden staves hooped with metal, and with two ears or handles, sometimes with silver mountings, or made entirely of silver; now mainly ornamental.
red biddy *slang* a mixture of cheap red wine and methylated spirit or other alcohol.
riddle a measure of claret, thirteen bottles arranged round a **magnum (bonum).**
shilling used until the 1950s in the classification of the strength of beer, from the price per barrel, *eg* **forty·shilling ale** (*usually written* 40/·) a very light beer; later re-introduced (without reference to the price) in the 'real-ale' boom of the 1970s.
skoosh a splash, sput, jet of liquid; lemonade or other aerated water.
slock yer drooth quench your thirst.
special *of beer* applied to a later carbonated version of **heavy.**
stowp a flagon, tankard, decanter, mug, often with its capacity, *eg* **pint stowp:** the measure itself.
tappit hen a kind of (usually pewter) decanter containing a standard measure (its knob resembling a fowl's tuft).
usquebae old name for whisky.
weet the bairn's heid toast the birth of a newborn baby.
weet yer thrapple have something to drink, quench your thirst.
wersh 1 tasteless, insipid. 2 bitter, harsh in taste, sour.
whisky a spirit distilled from malted barley in a pot still (**malt whisky**), or with the addition of unmalted grain spirit (usually maize) made in a patent still (**blended whisky**).

*Extracted from **The Scots Thesaurus,** to be published in 1990 by Aberdeen University Press for the Scottish National Dictionary Association.*

ACKNOWLEDGEMENTS

I would like to thank the editors of the different areas of the city: Andrew Marshall and Aileen McColgan who did Leith, James Haliburton and Craig McLean who did the Old Town, David Stenhouse who did the Southside, Desie Fahy and Eileen who did the west of Edinburgh, and Will Meldrum who did the New Town.

Our publishers need thanking for risking their time and money on a book written by the most unreliable authors: students. It is our hope that Polygon will continue to encourage students to pursue publishing projects.

The Guide was compiled and edited in the back room of Sue Simpson's new house. This remarkable lady managed to type all of the manuscripts, provide tea, biscuits and pizza for the editors, bring up a small child and pursue a university education at the same time without once getting in a flap. Thanks very much to you and your husband, Bob, for the use of your house and for your amazing patience.

The individual contributors, who braved the angry venom of antagonistic landlords and the drunken over-enthusiasm of the regulars to provide the information for the reviews, are the ones who are responsible for the book and therefore should have the most thanks: Rupert Boissier, Henry Golding, Ian Banks, Hamish Henderson, Christian Orr-Ewing, Magnus, Paula Collins, Jerry Corrish, John Martin, Fionna McKinnon, Paul Becket, Loretta Bresciani, Eddie Campbell, Oliver Carl, Ben Carver, Tim Daniels, Ben Duncan, Ian MacIntosh, Cathy Milton, Philip Parr, Chris Young, Mike Nash, Tom Lappin, Alun Graves, J.T., Emma Simpson, Pru Jeffreys, Andrew Sparrow, Graeme Wilson, Briony Sergeant, Sung, Jenifer Beer, Alison Smith, M.B., Kenny MacLeod.

And to those who provided the photographs and graphics, thank you: Pud, Kirsty Morrison, Will Meldrum, Fergus, Tiddy Maitland-Titterton, Susan Malvern, Lucy, Inki, Hugh Pinney, Torquil Crammer, Kenneth Simpson.

Finally I would like to thank John Stevenson-Hamilton who managed the advertising, Billy Kay who helped with good advice at the planning of this book, Charlie McMasters of the Heriot Watt University Brewing Archive who helped with much of the background material and Gillian Waugh who designed it all.